POOR RICHARD'S HORSE KEEPER

Poor Richard's Horse Keeper

More ways than a poor soul can count to save time
and money providing quality care for horses today

By

SUSAN McBANE

with

BENJAMIN FRANKLIN

For information, address:
Breakthrough Publications
Ossining, New York 10562

Cover and text design by Jacques Chazaud

Printed in the United States of America

Library of Congress Catalog Card Number: 93-73041

ISBN 0-914327-52-6

99 98 97 96 95 8 7 6 5 4 3 2

This book is dedicated to

ROY

a working horse owner who never seems
to have any time or money

Contents

Preface

I'm so pleased to be presenting this book to American readers—with the "help" of Benjamin Franklin (a real American name on both sides of the Atlantic).

We in Britain have admired the extremely high standards of riding and horse care shown by visiting American teams and individual competitors. Although some of our techniques and practices are different, a horse is a horse is a horse, whether he lives in the UK or the USA, and we all have the best interests of our horses at heart. I hope, therefore, that American readers will appreciate the sentiment that runs through this book—of trying to ensure the horse's well-being—and will find that we have much more common ground than differences in the ways of achieving this goal.

This book was written mainly for working horse owners, that increasingly large group of people who must work not only to keep themselves but also to keep their horse or horses. Because they work, many people simply do not have time to complete all the tasks they deem necessary for a horse's proper care. I find that many people become tied down by other people's standards—particularly those set by national equestrian organizations—and try to run their horse-life by other people's ideas of what is good and bad horse management. Many of us in Britain are too conformist for our horses' and our own good, too worried about doing things "by the book," and are consequently rushed off our feet most of the time as we try to squeeze in a career, a horse, domestic responsibilities, family, and some kind of social life. I know things are much the same in America. For several years, both our countries have been experiencing a recession, and economies in time and money have become more important than ever.

I do hope American readers will find the book as encouraging, helpful, and down-to-earth as British readers tell me they have found it. It *is* possible to juggle a job, family, social life, and horses without any of them suffering, and this book will show you how. The section on prioritizing is probably the most important in the book from the perspective of saving time. It is the key to keeping a horse truly well cared for on limited time and money.

The nuggets of wisdom offered *a la* Benjamin Franklin are intended as gentle yet succinct reminders of essential points.

Finally, I truly hope and believe that this book will help you to stay sane among the substantial demands of your life!

Acknowledgments

I should first like to thank Sue Triggs for executing the line drawings which have enhanced this book and have provided both explanation and decoration. She has depicted actual facilities known to the author but which she herself has not seen and has done an excellent job under less than ideal conditions. Anthony Crossley also readily provided ideas and information concerning his own system of management which have been incorporated in the book.

I must give special thanks to my American editor, Emily Kilby, who has been invaluable in helping me adapt this book for U.S. readers and in creating the mottoes in the style of Benjamin Franklin. Finally, I should like to express my appreciation to Daniel DeWeese for his superb photographs—which bring life to many of the ideas expressed in this book—and to the following facilities where many of the photographs were taken: Cedar Ridge Arabians, Jordan, MN; Horseshoe Lake Arabians, Stillwater, MN; Longview Ranch, Dayton, MN; and R-Style Arabians, Stacy, MN.

Susan McBane
September 1993

1

Managing Yourself and Your Horse

There is a very well-worn saying in the horse world and one which is very true: It says "each horse is an individual and must be treated as such." It is also true that there are certain set methods and procedures of horse care which are widely accepted and used and which are detailed in most good books on horse management. Somewhere between the individuality of a particular horse and the uniform method of a set management system lies the secret of keeping a horse happy, healthy and well cared for.

> **Content makes poor men rich; discontent makes rich men poor.**

When a horse owner can spend only limited time looking after a horse because of work and other commitments, it is particularly important that the horse is kept in a compatible management system. The otherwise-occupied owner will not always be there to cater to the horse's needs if the animal is not very happy about something. It is no use, for example, trying to make an active, athletic type of horse who is always full of energy (nervous or otherwise) exist under a system where he spends twenty-three out of his twenty-four hours stabled. It would also be somewhat unsatisfactory to keep turned out the type of animal who curls up at the first sign of wind or rain.

Let us, therefore, look at the various systems of horse management, the advantages and disadvantages of each and how we can relate them to horses' differing constitutions and temperaments.

Stabling Keeping a horse entirely or almost entirely stabled is obviously the most binding and time-consuming management option. It is not, however, necessarily much more expensive than other forms

Every horse is an individual and deserves to be treated as such.

There are various ways to keep horses and ponies without using strictly conventional stable complexes. This drawing shows a mare and foal in what used to be loose housing for young cattle. It has undergone no conversion at all, other than the broken glass windows being replaced with plexiglass. The wooden hayracks separating the "stalls" give large communal supplies of hay, which can be reached by animals on both sides. The horses can see each other through the bars, increasing their sense of company. Under the racks run the original mangers, which catch bits of hay that might otherwise fall to the floor and be wasted. (The haynets shown can provide a supplementary supply, although they are not actually recommended for foals who might, in their antics, catch a hoof in the mesh.) This sort of stabling is ideal for loose housing of several temperamentally compatible animals. The entrances are in an aisle to the right, out of the picture, and caretakers have the advantage of working under cover in this little unit. This is an excellent example of providing good housing without major construction expense.

of keep. Facilities for less work-intensive systems, such as acreage for pasturing a herd, may still have to be rented, for instance. Corralled horses have to be fed as stabled horses all year round, and in winter pasture-kept horses will probably need more food than stabled ones to withstand the cold.

A stabled horse has to have everything done for him by his human attendants, so time and convenience will be at a premium. The minimum daily caretaking includes

• at least two hours of exercise, which does not necessarily mean ridden or driven exercise, but general moving about either at will or being led, lunged or long-reined, as the case may be;

- grooming to prevent excessive buildup of dandruff and grease in his coat as he is not exposed to rain;

- stall cleaning, not only to maintain physical hygiene but also for the horse's mental health as horses in general dislike being near their own droppings;

- regular and frequent small feedings to maintain the horse's digestive health;

- possibly looking after blankets and other items of horse "clothing."

It may be very difficult for an owner with limited time to see to all the needs of a stabled horse, particularly the exercise requirement.

Among the advantages of keeping a horse stabled are

- the relative ease of keeping him clean, as he will not be able to coat himself in mud,

- his constant and convenient availability,

- the potential for keeping him fit, as compared to grass-kept horses (although corral-kept horses can be just as fit);

- the capability for minutely controlling his diet, an important consideration for horses in physically demanding work who cannot perform at their optimum level when consuming too much grass.

> **At least two hours of exercise a day keep ill health and boredom at bay.**

Keeping a Horse on Pasture

Seen by many as the most natural system of horsekeeping, the outdoor life does, however, have disadvantages as well as advantages for both horse and owner.

On the plus side, "outdoor" horses can

- exercise themselves at will, although they tend not to do so when miserable,

- eat grass when hungry and drink whenever thirsty (a source permitting),

- enjoy the company of their own kind and develop natural social relationships in most cases.

Stabled and otherwise-isolated horses, such as stallions, aren't able to enjoy all these natural pleasures and advantages. From

Outdoor horses can exercise at will and graze whenever they're hungry.

their attendants' point of view, such horses are not quite as demanding as stabled horses, although it is best if they are seen twice daily to check on their general well-being, for feeding if necessary and so that action can be taken in case of accidents, kicks and the like. A certain amount of grooming needs to be done—at least, discharges from eyes and nostrils should be assessed and sponged away, feet picked out and shoes, if worn, checked and blankets or rugs, when worn, frequently readjusted and changed.

Year-round pasturing may not suit every horse and owner. Some breeds of horse, such as Thoroughbreds, Arabs and other Oriental types originating in hot climates, may not thrive outdoors in cold, wet, windy weather. Such thin-skinned animals are prone not only to exposure in winter but to unbearable attacks from insects in summer. Some animals suffer badly from mud fever and rain rot when conditions are right and, despite run-in sheds and New Zealand rugs, simply cannot stand being out in a cold field.

> **Winter cold exacts its toll in clothing costs or feeding bills.**

This shows a top-quality field shelter of a type sold by many stabling manufacturers. It is located on the highest, and therefore the driest, part of the field with its back to the prevailing wind. A partial wall in the front would contribute to all-round shelter for when the wind changes direction but would also create a corner in which one animal might trap another. The shelter is maintained in deep-litter bedding, and the long hayrack running along the back is kept stocked with hay except when the grazing is plentiful in late spring, summer and early autumn. This shelter has gutters and a downspout to take the rainwater which would otherwise drip down the front and onto the horses if, like many, they have the habit of standing half in and half out the shed. There is no drain to take the water, as it drains away naturally. The shelter is built on a layer of bricks to help protect the lower timbers from the damp ground. Even simpler shelters can be built using a single-pitch roof that slopes from front to back, obviating the need for guttering and downspouts. However, this arrangement allows in more "weather." Second-hand lumber can be used and haynets provided instead of the hayrack. No matter what other cost-cutting measures are taken, the choice of building site (high and dry; back to the prevailing wind) and entrance design (high, wide and welcoming with room to allow the most pick-upon member of the herd to escape) should be the same for every horse shed constructed.

Compared to stabled horses, even the best adapted pasture-kept horses will be

- harder to keep fit when they're grazing on lush grass;

- more difficult to keep clean, especially in wet weather (which is unlikely to worry them but may worry their owners);

- stressed by harsh winter weather, causing them to eat more feed to maintain body condition;

- inconvenient to care for outdoors during bad weather unless they can be tied up in a shelter or somewhere under cover.

Many horse keepers have found the combination of stabling and turnout to be ideal.

The Combined System

The combination of stabling and turnout is considered by many authorities to be the best approach to keeping horses. The system is very flexible, with the number of hours in and out varying according to daily circumstances.

The combined system works very well indeed because the horse can have the freedom of an outdoor life but with the warmth and shelter of his stable, when needed. He can be kept as fit as any stabled horse, but because he can also be turned out he is not as demanding of his owner as a stabled animal. Feed and bedding can be saved according to time of year and length of time the horse is turned out each day.

The combined system is ideal for avoiding those extremes of both the other systems with their attendant problems—exposure and cold in winter in susceptible individuals and excess heat and insect attacks in summer with the outdoor system, and the boredom, frustration and inner tension, resulting in various vices and other physical and mental problems, which can occur when horses are kept fully stabled even when they are given what we consider to be adequate exercise.

Horses rarely appreciate extremes of either of the first two systems, in my experience. Because of its obvious practical advantages, I am a great fan of the combined system.

> **If you care for your horse, put his freedom before your convenience.**

Yarding   "Yarding" is another system increasingly used in Great Britain and Ireland. It is used not only for breeding stock and resting horses but also for horses in work. Horses are kept in dirt enclosures, partly or fully roofed, and so have the freedom to exercise themselves as much as space will allow but with the advantage of significant shelter. Sometimes the enclosure is a yard in front of a large, open-fronted shed which is bedded down, and the horse or horses can come and go as they wish. In other cases, a single stall may have a smaller yard leading from it, which simply permits the horse to walk about and have a measure of freedom.

Facilities used vary considerably, and the system has much to recommend it because it gives horses some freedom without the disadvantages of their being out on pasture. The dirt yards normally used will not support grass in any quantity, so horses have to be fed as stabled horses.

"Corralling" is a system used in the United States and some other countries and is closely allied to yarding except that the

"Almost anything is better than being stabled all the time." This picture shows two former bull stalls and their attached pens, which were successfully converted to horse stabling. The doors are left open nearly all the time; the horses wear appropriate blankets when weather conditions demand and spend most of their time outdoors. Access to the box stalls is through side doors, there being no gates in the walls of the pens. Windows in the back stall walls, the side windows, and the top doors are left open for ventilation, according to conditions. Although the pens are only slightly bigger than the stalls, they provide the horses with that much extra room and remove the sense of imprisonment which so many stabled horses experience. There is everything to be said for providing such a facility in suitable locations in front of existing stables, perhaps with an access gate in the front wall of the pen where there is only one door in the stall. Ordinary fencing could, of course, be used instead of brick and iron bars.

horses may not have shelter. They are kept in a high-fenced pen and fed by their attendants as stabled horses but do have the freedom to exercise themselves. The corral is also often used for schooling purposes.

The choice of a suitable system depends on several things. Most important of these is your horse's constitution and temperament. As briefly mentioned earlier, neither of you will be happy if you choose the wrong method. If you have a high-strung horse always wanting to be on the go, but you have the time to give him only an hour or two of work each day, it will not be surprising if he develops one or more stable vices or other mental or physical problems should you decide to keep him more or less fully stabled. On the other hand, a thin-skinned, hot-blooded type of animal will be thoroughly miserable and will suffer considerably, mentally and physically, if he is wintered out without proper facilities—shelter, clothing and ample feeding—and maybe even with them.

It would be helpful if we could say what breeds and types do best under what systems, but there is so much individual variance that the only reliable advice which can be given is "know your own horse." There are many Thoroughbred and Arab-type horses who winter out happily given good facilities. Likewise, just because a more cold-blooded type of horse is normally regarded as a placid animal, not particularly sensitive to the elements and not inclined to be on the go all the time, it does not mean that all crossbreds and ponies, for example, can live out with equanimity year round or, conversely, stay happily stabled most of the time on limited exercise.

It is essential to really get to know your horse as an individual, to understand his mental and physical needs and tendencies, so that you can try to accommodate him in the most suitable way. Unhappy horses do not thrive and can cost more to keep than contented ones. Those who develop vices, such as cribbing, wind-sucking and eating foreign matter (e.g. wood and droppings), often have digestive troubles as well, which mean food is not being utilized as well as it could be. This is a waste of money, and such vices can actually lead to colics that add the further expense of veterinary bills. Confined horses who take up other vices, such as weaving and stall walking, may, again, be poor doers, not least because they are using physical energy all the time. On the other hand, horses exposed to cold, wet conditions may expend tremendous energy just trying to keep warm—again, a waste of money which stabling and a good rug would obviate.

Which System for You and Your Horse?

> **Unhappy horses do not thrive and cost more to keep than contented ones.**

This picture shows how one end of a covered hay barn has been adapted as a run-in shed connected with an adjoining paddock. The horses cannot reach the stored bales but have their own supply of hay provided in racks around the perimeter. This facility provides for the horses' physical and mental needs, and their owner finds them easily cared for. Both horses compete actively in amateur shows yet are very rarely stabled. They wear turnout blankets and are trace clipped in winter. The horses remain as fit as when they were kept stabled in their previous accommodation, but their care is considerably less demanding for their owner.

Let the horse's needs guide you in choosing the right management system. As a working owner, particularly one without his or her own facilities who has to keep a horse on someone else's premises, either at a boarding stable or in rented accommodation, you may have few horse-keeping options. But I feel it is better to seek peace of mind for both of you and to keep your horse, say, a little further from your home than you would normally wish and know he is being cared for according to his requirements, than to have him close by but forced to put up with conditions that make him unhappy and worry you.

Your own working hours, domestic commitments and the length of your commute to and from work will also have a bearing on just how much time you can spend on your horse and will, therefore, govern to some extent the management system you adopt. I would venture to suggest, however, that if your time availability, or lack of it, is such that you cannot spare the four hours or so a day it takes to exercise, groom, muck out, feed and otherwise look after a fully stabled horse, then do not consider this system of management. Nor, in fact, would you be wise to own the type of horse who cannot stand to be out in winter for long hours while you are at work. If the horse is miserable, he will not exercise himself and so help to keep himself warm but, instead, will mope by the gate, getting colder and colder and more and more unhappy, until you or someone else appears to bring him in.

Only you can really assess the situation, depending on your horse and your other circumstances.

Although at-home care is the arrangement of choice for the majority of Americans, many horse and pony owners keep their animals on someone else's property. They do so usually because they lack the necessary facilities—land, stabling, feed, storage, and so forth—at home, but some choose a boarding situation because they are unable or unwilling to give the time and commitment to daily horse care. Such owners, therefore, board their horses, most often at a riding school or boarding stable. There is a method which comes between these two systems, and that is doing your horse yourself but not at home—that is, in a rented accommodation. Let us look at these three sources of accommodation.

Where to Keep Your Horse

At Home

For many owners, this is the best way to keep a horse. It is much more convenient, certainly, than having to travel to your horse, and you can normally be sure that no one is "tampering" with him while you are not present. Because you, and possibly other family members, look after him yourselves, you can be certain that he is cared for according to your requirements.

However, if you are keeping your horse at home and looking after him entirely yourself, with no family help, it is extremely demanding, unless you can get occasional, possibly paid, help when you are ill or away.

If you do not have suitable facilities at home they will have to be created, but, of course, your local zoning and building regulations have the final say on your options. Horses, considered livestock rather than pets under land-use regulations, are banned outright by some local codes, are restricted by others and specifically exempted from agricultural status by yet others. Building codes may specify lot size or site placement for stable construction, and increasingly stringent environmental regulations may detail what you can and cannot do with your manure pile, your potential pasture and any "wetlands" on your property.

Before looking at the first stable plan or buying the first plank, consult your local zoning board and building code about the

> **If you'd have a servant that you like, serve yourself.**

requirements for keeping horses on your property. Consult with your lawyer, as well, if you have the slightest confusion about the regulations and requirements. When you come to erect the stable, you will need plans and expert advice as to the actual siting of it and on health and safety matters. Basically, though, you will have to pay attention to such things as

- drainage, insects and odors,

- fire risks where hay, straw or other inflammable materials are on site,

- heavy-truck traffic for delivery of feed and bedding,

- secure fencing to keep horses on your property and trespassers out.

Even taking into account the expense of providing at-home facilities, your day-to-day costs will be less than keeping the horse anywhere else because you will have no rent or board charges to pay. And, of course, the stable or stables and ancillary buildings will add to the value of your property if they are well and tastefully constructed (and to your property-tax bill, as well!).

If you live in a residential area, you will have to give serious thought to manure disposal. In fact, if you can put the actual droppings straight into sacks which you then staple or tape up ready for sale (or giving away, if you must), you will obviate many of the problems of flies and smells which go with manure piles. The used bedding, minus droppings, could be used as footing in an exercise area, if you have room. Alternatively, you could arrange with a local nursery or market gardener to take the manure away very frequently. In this case, the heap will have to be located not only as far from houses as possible but where the removal truck can get to it.

From the horse's point of view, the main disadvantages of living at your home may be limited turnout facilities and lack of company. You may be able to remedy the first by means of plenty of under-saddle exercise and by providing an area just big enough for him to have a good roll and kick up his heels when he wants; almost anything is better than being stabled all the time. Lack of company may not be so easy to cope with, and your horse may form a friendship with your family dog or some other animal.

It is better to give him other equine company if at all possible, perhaps by renting a stall to a friend. Or you may be able to kill two problems with one stone by renting pasture or turnout space

> **To you perfume;
> to neighbors
> a noisome stink.**

from a nearby horse owner with a larger acreage than you have. Many horses live quite happily if they are turned out on nearby grazing with other horses, just coming home to solitary stabling at night or whenever needed.

At a Boarding Stable

Time is money, and it is sometimes necessary to spend one in order to save the other. With boarding arrangements, you are spending money to save time. In theory at least, if you are paying full-board charges for your horse there should never be any actual need for you to go and see him at all; you do so simply because you want to see him and be with him or to ride or drive him.

Different stables have different ideas of what constitutes full board, but it should include stabling, bedding, grooming, feeding and watering and adequate exercise according to the horse's state of health and fitness. I feel that, when the option exists, grazing should be included in the fees because, although it does cost money to maintain grazing, most stables save on feed when horses are out on pasture, even if on just one feed/hay ration a day. However, many stables charge extra for grazing and many do not give enough exercise, seeming to regard one hour a day, and nothing else, as adequate. In practice, many stables will exercise your horse four days a week, assuming you will be riding two days—weekends, normally—and the horse will be having one day off. So all the exercise some boarded horses get is four hours a week, which is not very much by anyone's standards. If the horse can be turned out for at least half of each day in addition, this might suffice. Otherwise it will be quite inadequate to maintain a horse in reasonable mental and physical health.

If you want more exercise, assuming it is available in terms of manpower and time, you will have to pay for it. If the stable has a mechanical horse-walker, this will at least stretch the horse's legs and should cost a bit less than "personal" exercise. The machine can exercise upwards of four horses at once, depending on design, and requires only one person to supervise. As with lunging, half an hour on a walker is enough for any horse.

You will have to pay extra for shoeing, schooling, veterinary expenses, tack and other equipment (although not normally such equipment as pitchforks and rakes) and also, where appropriate, traveling costs, plus insurance. While tack cleaning is often included in the standard boarding fee, clipping and show preparation are usually extra. You may have to pay a fee for the use of a cross-country course, show jumps, an indoor school or other

> **Time is money, and it is sometimes necessary to spend one in order to save the other.**

exercise facilities for a given number of hours.

When investigating a possible stable for your horse,

• ask if there are any charges in addition to the standard boarding fee;

• check the security of the tack room and stable in general, as thefts of horses and equipment are on the increase;

• examine the stable flooring to see that it's well-maintained, safe and comfortable for the horses who must stand on it for hours and hours daily;

• look at the safety of both the indoor or outdoor exercise areas, checking for broken or missing fencing boards, stones, uneven going, holes and excessive dust.

• inquire about the daily schedule, particularly any time restrictions on your using or visiting your horse.

At the time of writing, full-board charges vary, according to the area of the country and proximity to urban centers, from roughly $150 to $700 per month.

Partial board is cheaper, obviously, because you get fewer services. Most partial-board clients simply choose stabling, grazing, bedding, feeding and watering and skip all grooming services, exercising and tack cleaning.

When you board your horse at a riding center, you will be charged less if you allow your horse to be used "in the school," that is for students and selected clients to ride or drive. Unfortunately, it often works out that they need your horse when you want him; also, it is never good for a horse to have too many people working him, especially novices, so such arrangements should be gone into with care.

Good boarding stables are extremely rare in some areas, and many owners are in the unfortunate position of having to take more or less what they can get. However, as mentioned earlier, it is worth a small fortune in peace of mind to keep your horse further away from home at a good place rather than at a poorer one closer by.

> **Better to drive far for peace of mind than stay near for cheapness.**

To assess a stable, simply judge the condition of the horses, not only their physical condition but their mental attitude, as well:

• Are they correctly fed or thin or over-fat?

• Are they reasonably clean even when out of work or have they obviously not had a brush or sponge near them for days?

• Are they calm and interested in their surroundings, with contented, alert expressions, or are they miserable looking, not bothering to look out of their stalls; indeed, are they able to look out of their stalls?

• Do too many of them show obviously suspect temperaments?

As for their general management, check out the following aspects of their care:

• Is the bedding thick and clean, whatever material is used?

• Are the stalls light and airy with plenty of room for each animal to lie fully flat out (necessary for deep sleep), get up and turn around in comfort?

• Is there uneaten feed, particularly hay? If so, is it good quality and the horses have simply had quite enough for the time being, or is it poor and/or sour, so that the horses will leave it even though they are still hungry and resort to eating foreign substances, such as wood, droppings and bedding?

• Are the water containers and the water in them clean.

• Are blankets clean and well fitting?

Slight untidiness in the stable yard or tack room, woodwork in need of painting and a less-than-immaculate manure pile do not matter much. Hopefully, this shows that more attention is paid to the horses themselves than to matters which do not directly affect the horses.

Human relationships at the boarding stable are important, too. You could find life somewhat difficult if you keep your horse at a place run by people you cannot talk to or do not much like. Approachable, understanding, trustworthy, knowledgeable people are well worth seeking out. Remember, a bad atmosphere in a stable due to poor personal relationships may affect the horses, who can certainly sense it, and the level of attention

---

**When a friend deals with a friend,
Let the bargain be clear and well penn'd,
That they continue friends to the end.**

and care paid to them; their sense of security could well be affected to the detriment of their well-being.

In a Communal Boarding Barn

"Do-it-yourself" boarding is simply a term for keeping your horse in rented accommodation and caring for him entirely yourself. You simply pay for stabling and, possibly separately, the pasture and buy all your own feed, bedding and equipment. You are solely responsible for the day-to-day care of your horse. Such arrangements are the next cheapest alternative to keeping your horse at home but take up more time and generate more expenses than having the horse outside your own back door because of the travel involved in visiting the horse at least twice a day. That is unless you're fortunate enough to have the boarding barn next door. These do-it-yourself arrangements seem to be becoming more and more common as keep and board charges rise faster than salaries, and Chapter 4 deals with communal boarding and renting schemes in which friends and families help each other out with the work involved.

> Trust thyself, and another shall not betray thee.

When checking out an accommodation for such an arrangement, the facilities—stabling, grazing and individual storage areas for each client, not to mention a decent, secure tack room—are really what matter, as the condition of the individual horses and ponies present is controlled by their owners. However, if you visit a place where the animals largely seem not to be too well cared for, perhaps you should look elsewhere. Not only are these the type of owners on whom you might have to rely for help more or less frequently, but the state of their animals might well get on your nerves to the extent that your own contentment and satisfaction with your lot are adversely affected—it certainly does happen.

It may be possible to get your horse cared for and accommodated free or simply for the cost of his feed and bedding if he acts as companion to another horse. Many owners who work alone would welcome some part-time help too, and you could come to a mutual agreement over stable work for the benefit of you and your horses.

You may be lucky enough to find premises rent free if you undertake to put and keep them in good repair. Although no money changes hands in this sort of deal, a written agreement would be a good idea to protect both parties' interests. If you are of the entrepreneurial type, you could rent a stable and then charge others for stabling, not only covering your costs but

When choosing a stable, consider the people who run it and work there, too. You and your horse will benefit from knowledgeable, understanding treatment.

making a profit as well, particularly if you can act as manager.

Finally, when choosing a stable, consider the location. If you want to spend your time hacking rather than riding in a ring, for instance, it is no use stabling your horse in the middle of an asphalt jungle or surrounded by dangerous roads. Or if you wish to improve your and your horse's prowess across country, it could be inconvenient if there is no facility for cross-country riding either on the premises or nearby.

Income and Expenditure

Ultimately, your goal is to weigh all the factors and try to end up with your horse at your home or in a stable

> **Necessity never made a good bargain.**

- where he will be well cared for by you, by staff or by other owners, friends or family members,

- with the facilities required for your particular equestrian discipline,

- which is conveniently located,

- which is not too expensive for your income.

It is usually worth paying a little extra for what you want and being happy, rather than scrimping and saving small amounts and ending up in an unsatisfactory arrangement.

2

A Year in Your Life: An Overview

The equestrian sporting year never ends but simply turns full circle. Different equestrian disciplines have their seasons, and some, notably show jumping and, to a lesser extent, local-level showing, are simply divided into an indoor season in winter and an outdoor season in summer. For the owner of the "all-purpose" horse, there are more than enough equestrian activities to take part in to keep horse and rider occupied all year round.

The Seasons of the Year

In spring some hunting will still be going on, the show season has started with its various ring-judged disciplines along with ancillary events such as gymkhanas. The sports of eventing, endurance riding and combined driving will have their spring seasons. Point-to-points and steeplechasing have spring meets, although this is hardly a suitable outlet for most "ordinary" horses and their owners.

> **Look ahead, or you'll find yourself behind.**

Summer sees polo joining the scene, while the more demanding cross-country sports are put out to pasture because of the season's high temperatures and generally hard footing. Of course, trail riding purely for pleasure picks up considerably with the lengthening of daylight hours and the arrival of temperate weather.

In autumn, cub hunting will start, and there is the fall season for eventing, driving trials and endurance riding. For many breeds and activities, autumn brings the culminating shows of the year—the nationals where year-end awards and championships are decided.

Winter sees hunting proper in full swing or avid competitors getting their mounts fit for spring events of various kinds. There are local shows (indoor and out), Pony Club and 4-H events, private driving, hunter trials, dressage and instructional courses and clinics. For those who just like to ride for the fun of it, without competing or hunting, there is, of course, hacking all year round, and hacking can be as placid or strenuous as you want it to be, depending, admittedly, on local facilities.

The Advantages of Year-Round Fitness

Whatever work your horse is to do, he has to be made fit and to be cared for appropriately for the task in hand. This book is not a manual on the specific topic of caring for horses, but on how to save time and money in doing so. Readers are assumed to have a reasonable standard of knowledge, therefore, but perhaps a few words on the difficulties and advantages presented by each season of the year and how they affect our preparation for various disciplines will not go amiss.

It is worth noting, first, that it takes less time and effort to keep a horse fit than to actually get him fit. The type of horse mainly under consideration in this book—the all-round, family-type or amateur-owner horse—will probably get enough work throughout the year to remain, say, three-quarters fit (if we take fully fit as racing or three-day-eventing fit). This is a considerable advantage because this type of fitness is quite adequate for what you will want him to do and can be maintained by the horse's normal work plus a bit extra. It is also better for his general health to be always partially fit like this than to be allowed to get fat and soft in summer or thin and rundown in winter.

To restore a horse to reasonable fitness from either of those two conditions requires a lot of time, slow work, patience, skill in feeding and judgment of his changing physical condition. Without those qualities, it is easy to overstress an unfit horse and end up with legs or lungs that won't withstand the season because they weren't given enough slow roadwork at the beginning of a fitness program.

The horse who is always fairly fit is less susceptible to stresses and strains during the normal course of his work. He is also healthier, provided his general care is correct and appropriate, and less prone to work-related accidents and even to accidents in the field. Because his body is "tuned up," he can use it better to get out of scrapes, such as uneven ground or a tree which suddenly looms up and needs dodging or a companion who decides to have a mad half-hour and chivvy everybody else in the paddock.

There is, of course, no substitute for acquiring as much knowledge as possible and being able to manage one's horse or horses under all conditions and in all states of well-being, but generally speaking a horse who is fairly fit and in work most of the year is less of a liability to his owner than one whose condition varies significantly with the seasons.

> **Better a part-fit horse throughout the year, than one who goes from soft to hard to soft again.**

The Woes of Winter

For most working owners and their horses, at least those living outside the Sun Belt states, winter is the most difficult time of year. The worst part of winter, apart from the dark which makes exercising difficult, is cold rain. If you try to exercise the horse, you'll both get soaked—unless, of course, you have access to an indoor arena. The wet also often brings with it rain rot and scratches (dealt with in Chapter 7) and often makes turnout facilities, particularly small, overcrowded or badly drained ones, unusable due to the pocked, slippery surface or simply standing water.

Wet combined with cold and wind can have a very serious chilling effect on horses with inadequate shelter, even when they are well fed. Such conditions are just as miserable for the human side of the partnership, although both can obtain a good deal of

> **Though the work be even the whole year round, a stabled horse's keep is woeful hard in winter, mere breeze in summertime.**

protection and comfort from well-fitting waterproof clothing.

You will certainly have your work cut out for you caring for a clipped, grain-fed horse adequately in winter if you are also working and/or have other time-consuming commitments such as looking after a house and family. If you have a nine-to-five job, it may only just be getting light when you have to leave the horse and set off for work, and it will certainly be dark again when you return. Somehow, exercising on light summer evenings doesn't seem like a chore at all, whereas the same task during identical hours on a dark winter night is exactly that. A stabled, grain-fed horse involves just as much work, winter and summer, but in winter that work does seem more onerous!

There are, of course, dangers inherent in taking out a horse on public roads after dark although, as discussed in Chapter 7, much can be done to lessen them. However, many owners feel that their winter burden is lightened if their horse can be turned out during the time they are at work, even if only for a few hours a day.

There may be times in winter when freezing conditions make road exercise or any other ridden or driven exercise almost impossible, so this can create more work in the way of laying down manure tracks for riding or lunging on, and then clearing them away again when the thaw comes.

If the weather freezes significantly, rather than just hovering around freezing point, this can, in fact, make turnout areas more acceptable. Horses used to daily turnout are normally quite safe if turned onto frozen fields as, being accustomed to being out, they will not go charging about like lunatics. They quickly sense the state of the ground and move accordingly.

Freezing weather sometimes creates major difficulties in watering horses, even stabled ones. Underground pipes need to be at least three feet deep if they are to escape the worst frosts, and those above ground have to be insulated. Horses in fields must have their water containers cleared of ice at least twice daily, and some horses refuse to drink out of a container which has broken ice floating on the top, anyway. If such horses have their water supplied by hose, you have to be sure to empty it out entirely after each use or bring it indoors each night; if water freezes inside it you will be left with no means of getting water to outdoor horses except by carrying buckets.

Come to think of it, I can find no actual advantages to winter except that there aren't any insects to bother the horses.

The Joys of Spring Spring, on the other hand, definitely does have advantages. Longer daylight hours make exercising safer and more pleasant, although it can still be very cold in spring. The main disadvan-

Springtime brings the joy of foals frolicking in the paddocks and pastures.

tage, once the grass starts coming through, is that if the grass is at all rich a surfeit can cause severe digestive and circulatory problems leading to colic and laminitis. Both conditions are very painful and incapacitating and can, in fact, lead to the death of the horse, either directly or because he's suffering so the owner decides to have him put down.

However, if the grass is of poor to medium quality and the horse is not totally unused to grass beforehand, long spring days out in the field while you are at work can be very pleasant for the horse and, as turning out usually is, laborsaving for you from the point of view of exercising.

Care should be taken during early spring to watch for sudden deterioration in the weather and to equip the horse with an appropriate weight, water-resistant blanket, if necessary, particu-

> **For all its goodness, beware the grass grown rich in spring.**

larly if he has been stabled and rugged up all winter. Otherwise, he will surely feel the cold and could lose condition.

The Two Sides of Summer

Summer can, in two particular respects, be as miserable for the horse as winter. First, there are the problems caused by flies. I am sure that most owners do not realize (and some simply ignore) the agonies that horses can go through when they are exposed to insects. It is worse during the daylight hours but there are night-flying insects, too, which bother horses.

Nature does equip horses with various anti-fly devices, such as manes and tails and an extensive flat muscle under the skin of the back, sides and flanks with which he can twitch flies off those areas. But to keep himself permanently free of their attentions, he must keep up a ceaseless performance of head shaking, leg stamping, muscle twitching and tail swishing, which is both mentally and physically wearying. In bad cases, flies drive horses to stampede around their paddocks, an exhausting and potentially damaging activity in the case of an unfit animal. As horses do not see well when galloping fast, it's also possible that they will collide with fencing, buildings, trees and other obstructions they would normally avoid, not least because their attention is more on the flies than on where they are going. Summer's hard ground also jars legs and breaks feet.

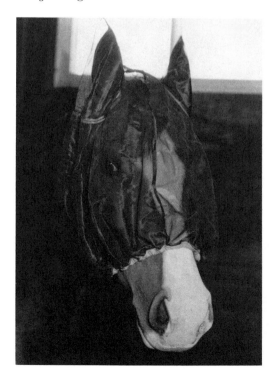

Flies, gnats, and mosquitoes plague horses during the warm summer months. Manure removal, insect repellents, and products like this fly mask help your horse keep comfortable.

A run-in shed in every horse paddock and pasture will protect horses from rain, snow, and even the sun. Such shelters are required by law in some states.

Sweet itch is a very distressing condition suffered in summer by horses allergic to the saliva of the *culicoides* midge, the "no-see-ums" that are active around sunrise and sunset. As treatment of established sweet itch is difficult, prevention—either application of effective repellents or stabling during the insects' active times—is the best approach to the problem. This applies to all insect problems, although it's virtually impossible to banish all bugs from horse premises.

The second main problem in what we humans call a good summer is sun and heat, which can distress horses considerably. Cool, shady areas provide a haven for them, particularly if they are out for many hours in daylight. This is the season when hard-working horses can succumb with surprising rapidity to dehydration, heat exhaustion and sunstroke.

Summer's benefits include the temperature, which many humans, particularly the sun seekers, love—no frozen fingers, cold rain or snow and ice to cope with. There is also no fretting over a hot horse getting chilled unless the weather is really unseasonal, no time-consuming blanketing and unblanketing, no being cluttered up with bulky clothing ourselves and, of course, there are

During summer's hot, turn your turnout inside out, making daytime night and nighttime day.

long evenings and light mornings which, together with the temperature, make horse management and the chores that go with the enjoyment much easier and more pleasant.

The Advantages of Autumn

Autumn brings a return to kinder conditions for horses. There are no extremes of heat or sun, insects gradually disappear and the ground softens, although in a very wet autumn, of course, it becomes muddy. The grass gives an autumn "flush" of growth, too, but it is of lower nutritional content, so if your horse is relying on grass for food at this time of year seek the advice of a specialist such as a veterinarian or equine nutritionist about the need for supplementation.

Nights start to draw in now, however, and blankets may be needed. And it is time of year when fog often creates problems. Although it might be permissible to exercise a horse in dusk or dark conditions if both rider and mount are suitably equipped with reflective clothing and a stirrup light (as discussed in Chapter 7), fog is a definite no-no as far as I am concerned for taking horses on to the road, even if they are lit up like Christmas trees; another means of exercising must be devised.

Vacations for Horse and Owner

Many horse owners plan their vacations around their equestrian activities, but others like a complete break away from all routine aspects of their normal lives. Those in the latter category obviously have to make arrangements for the care of their horses while they are away.

Holidays for horses usually mean a period at pasture so, from the horse's point of view, the best times of year to take a break are spring and/or autumn. Although the type of horse mostly being considered in this book may never be so tuned up that he becomes in dire need of a long rest, most horses do like to have a period on pasture with no work, provided it does not become too long and boring. A two-week break in spring and autumn to tie in with his owner's annual vacation seems ideal.

If you keep your horse at home and there is not going to be a suitably reliable, expert member of the family left there to care for him, it would be more satisfactory for him to be sent for the period in question to a reputable boarding stable or riding school. In fact, if a rest is not called for and money is not too tight,

> While the owner's away, will the horse have to pay?
> Better a two-week boarding bill than a neglected horse.

this would be a good opportunity for the horse to receive a period of professional schooling.

If you keep your horse in a do-it-yourself boarding stable, can you be absolutely certain that during your absence the other owners there will look after your horse in the manner to which he is accustomed, probably in exchange for your helping look after theirs in similar circumstances? If not, and you don't want the horse to go away to board, your only alternative might be to employ a free-lance groom to see to him morning and night while you are away.

Whatever arrangements you make, be sure that whoever is doing the honors while you are away has a telephone number where you can be reached in an emergency. If you are traveling, you should call up regularly and should, in any case, leave the caretaker the telephone number of your vet with authorization to call him or her, or any other vet of her choice in case yours is unavailable, should the need arise. The same goes for farriery problems—a neglected sprung or loose shoe can soon cause a nasty accident.

Also leave detailed feeding information and, if the horse is going away, a supply of his own food, particularly hay, so as not to cause digestive upsets which can come with a sudden change of feed.

The Conditioning Calendar

The basic preparation and conditioning for any equestrian activity is pretty much the same. If your horse is in work for most of the year, short breaks such as described above will not appreciably diminish his fitness, and you can subsequently carry on where you left off after perhaps just a few days' gentle work to help his mind and body get the message that it's back to normal now.

It is a good idea to sit down with a year planner and plot out the next twelve months. First put in the major events the horse is expected to attend and the dates of your vacations. Also put in the times of yearly medical checks, vaccinations, dental checks, blood tests or whatever are called for. Schedule these medical and dental procedures well before any of your planned events as many horses feel below par for some days afterwards, especially in the case of vaccinations. Dental work, too, can give a horse a sore mouth which may cause eating problems and a subsequent loss of energy and condition, not to mention biting difficulties. If the scheduled medical exam reveals a problem which needs attention, there will, hopefully, be time to deal with it before The Big Day if you've allowed adequate time while planning your yearly program.

With this basic information in front of you, you will have a clear

> **The year down on paper puts a purpose in your plans.**

picture of the horse's changing work pattern and, thus, of your own throughout the year. It does not always follow that when he is working hardest you will be too, for more rest days can be allowed so you will not necessarily be spending more time exercising. However, getting everything down on paper in an organized plan lets you see your year and what is involved more easily, enabling you to schedule your daily and weekly workloads to greatest advantage.

Consider, also, your precise method of management for each season in relation to the activities you are going to undertake. If you are going to spend the winter with the horse turned out during the day Monday through Friday and just hack about at weekends, does the horse really need clipping, even with a trace or Irish clip? An unclipped horse, with or without a turnout rug, can withstand long days out in the field while you are at work much better than a clipped one, and he'll need less food and clothing to keep him warm. However, if you are going to hunt on Saturdays and probably work the horse on a couple of weekdays to maintain fitness, too, some kind of clip will be needed to prevent excessive sweating and to facilitate care and cleaning afterwards.

In summer, when this category of horse normally works hardest, he will need to be quite fit for perhaps strenuous weekends and evening hacks or instructional classes. You have the daylight in your favor now, but if you should be in the position of having rich, plentiful grazing available, facilities will have to be secured and arrangements made to have the horse brought in for much of the time—say, during the day away from the flies—to reduce his grass intake. Otherwise, he will become too fat to do your work comfortably and safely, not to mention being at risk from the other problems of rich grazing.

By giving careful thought to your horse's individual constitution and temperament, both of which have an important bearing on his management, and to your own working times on a daily and yearly basis, plus the various equestrian activities you wish to take part in, you will be able to plan your year to best advantage. You'll also see quickly what is going to be involved during each season and so organize yourself accordingly.

Getting Fit for Different Disciplines

The key to fitness and to maintaining soundness, particularly leg soundness, in any horse is adequate preparation in the "slow" stages of a fitness program. This applies whether you are using interval training or traditional methods of conditioning a horse. A fitness program of whatever type, for whatever discipline, cannot be rushed. If it is skimped, it is simply not performed.

The type of program you use will depend on your horse's mental and physical constitution and the type of work he is going to do. For example, animals aimed at pursuits where hard, muscled-up fitness is not required can safely be given a slightly shorter walking period at the beginning of a fitness program. Two weeks instead of a month of walk work should be adequate for children's ponies and horses not doing much hard or fast work or a lot of jumping. Amateur showing, dressage, private driving and hacking come into this category.

For animals expected to do strenuous work, such as eventing, polo, racing of any kind, driving trials and endurance work, a month of walking work, culminating in about three hours a day with the horse walking properly up to his bridle most of the time, but with odd periods of relaxation, should be allowed and fitted into the year planner.

When trotting is introduced on roads it should be no more than a working trot. Some experts claim that no horse should trot on the road while others maintain that it helps harden legs and feet. My experience is that it is beneficial, and certainly not harmful, provided the trot is a steady one. If you have the kind of horse who will not walk on happily once he starts to get fit but wants to keep trotting before you feel he is ready, try to find softer ground for the trotting, such as road shoulders, fields, riding rings or the beach—whatever yielding footing is available to your circumstances. Again, provided the trotting is steady and limited in the early stages, it is better to let the horse trot on a bit and be happy than to keep nagging at him to slow down and perhaps spoil his urge to give you free, forward movement!

The further conditioning of your horse again depends on his job. The most time-consuming program is for the endurance horse as long rides must become part of his routine to harden and accustom him to bearing tack and weight for long periods. (He must also be trained to lead easily in hand for those spells when you travel off his back to rest it and to loosen up your own limbs.)

Racehorses of the various types will have short canters with the length, speed and frequency of workouts increasing until the horse is ready to race. His first race should bring him on in fitness, not take anything out of him. If it does, he was not ready for it. Event horses need to start specific dressage schooling and athletic jumping as well as long canters to build up stamina. Like endurance horses, they must become accustomed to covering the distances relevant to their competitive goals.

Horses in these categories may begin interval training proper at this stage, although few racehorses are conditioned by this method. The system does not lend itself to excitable horses, with

> **You must go slow before you can go fast.**

> **From part-way conditioned, each specialty takes its own route to full fitness.**

its constant stopping and starting, but can benefit and sharpen up the stuffier sorts.

Show jumpers, show horses and dressage horses need correct flat work to build up their muscles, develop obedience and develop their agility and "gymnastic" prowess. Like the eventers, jumpers also needing athletic jumping practice. It is often a good idea to combine hacks with dressage training to avoid the boredom of being "drilled." Even professional stables may not have a well-groomed riding ring or "formal" schooling area as such but instead use their own paddocks, local bridle paths and lanes for schooling. Under these circumstances, you can take advantage of every handy opportunity, such as the odd fallen tree or uneven ground, to develop balance, making sure the horse goes correctly round bends, bending in and out of trees and the like.

Training Turned-Out Horses

Provided the grass is not rich, the slow stage of a fitness program can certainly be carried out from the field. As his fitness increases and he's ready for the next stage, you can begin giving your horse a small feed of grain and hay on return, to gradually accustom the gut microbes to a change of food and allow those involved in the digestion of the new food to multiply. Early on in his training, there isn't even any need to get the horse shod. Given a strong set of hooves, he can comfortably do his walking in his field or on soft tracks if there are any. Short trips on hard, smooth roads will not harm him at all provided his feet are professionally trimmed and balanced. This working out of the field saves on shoeing, bedding and grooming and give the horse the opportunity to adapt gradually to his increasingly demanding working life.

The same basic principles apply whether the fitness program is starting in spring, summer, autumn or winter. Seasonal considerations do apply, of course, and in autumn or winter it may be easier to get the horse fit if he is clipped and given a turnout rug, depending on how thick his coat grows. In spring and summer, grass may have to be gradually restricted to effect a slimmer shape and allow for harder food to be fed—although many showing and dressage competitors seem to be competing for the Fattest Horse prize rather than the prize for the best conformed or the most agile, correct performance! The secret is obviously not yet out in some circles that obesity is not only ugly and damaging to health and performance but is also expensive to maintain.

> **Obesity is an expensive fashion.**

3
Money

There is very little you can do without money. Most people think they haven't got enough, and very few admit to having too much. It is noticeable that those who grumble that their money gives them nothing but problems never seem to divest themselves of it in quantities sufficient to bring them to the bread line! Money's advantages, it seems, definitely outweigh its disadvantages.

> **The use of money is all the advantage there is in having money.**

Unfortunately for us, horses come within the range of "expensive tastes." They are expensive animals to buy (yet not very profitable to sell unless you are producing world-class competition horses or bloodstock) and expensive to keep. There is nothing to be lost by cutting costs in horse keeping, provided the animals do not suffer, and everything to be gained by sensible and prudent economies. It might even mean the difference between keeping one horse or two or, indeed, having a horse at all.

Expenses can be cut drastically if you share a horse with someone else, although difficulties may arise over use and management. This is especially likely if you do not actually own a share in the horse but merely help pay the bills, and any sharing arrangement must be gone into very carefully, preferably with a written agreement on both sides.

For the amateur horse owner not out to actually earn a living from his or her horse, the only way to be financially prudent is to get and keep costs down and run the operation with a strict eye on the dollars and cents. True, competitions won can bring valued extra dollars into the kitty, but income from this source should be regarded as a bonus and not as an essential boost to the funds needed to keep the horse.

Earning Income from the Industry

If you happen to be willing and able to give lessons to other people, either on your horse or on theirs, you are officially classed as a self-employed instructor and should declare this income on your annual tax return. Should you make a habit of it, you are best advised to do the job properly and consult an accountant about the various implications. A good accountant will save you in tax more than his fee, which is also tax deductible.

For a start, an accountant will inform you that there are certain expenses you can claim against your "business," such as

> **Rare is the horseman who rides to wealth on his horse's back.**

- traveling to and from your clients,

- at least some of the maintenance of your horse (you will not be able to claim all his expenses as tax deductible against your business if the tax man construes that he was your private horse before you began instructing and that you still use him for enjoyment),

- some of your own horse-related expenses, such as your clothing and also transportation to shows, which could be regarded as a publicity operation to keep you in the public eye and attract business.

There are various advantages to being self-employed on a part-time basis in that losses in the horse business can be set against income from other sources, such as your main job, and against future profits. Unfortunately, you have to have the willpower to set aside regular amounts to cover federal and state quarterly self-employment taxes.

The whole scene of trying to make money out of your horse, or at least trying to make him pay for himself, is somewhat complicated, and if you are seriously considering trying it, you are strongly advised to consult the aforementioned accountant about all the financial implications. For instance, a horseperson whose only income derives from self-employment in the industry is faced with huge potential expenses—not all of which will be tax deductible—for insurance alone:

• health insurance to cover medical expenses and protect your income should you be ill or have an accident and be unable to earn,

• life insurance to protect your dependents, if appropriate, in the event of your death,

• liability insurance to cover you in the event of a claim against you for negligence or incompetence by one of your clients,

• a pension plan to provide for your old age and give you a standard of living above the poverty line.

If you're serious about self-employment to pay all or part of your way in the horse world, I recommend that you buy a few good books on the professional aspect of the horse business. Look at *Legal Forms, Contracts, and Advice for Horse Owners* by Sue Ellen Marder (Breakthrough) and *Tax Planning and Preparation for Horse Owners* by Sue Ellen Marder and Tony Winter (Breakthrough).

The "small" horse owner is unwise to actually rent out his or her horse as a hired hack without riding instruction. This is construed as running a riding establishment which has a set of regulations and liabilities of its own.

Before you start a wholesale cost-cutting operation, it is sensible to find out exactly, and truthfully, how much your horse is now costing you to keep over a period of a full year. Costs do vary according to the season. Many horses cost more to keep in winter because of the extra food needed in inclement weather, particularly working owners' horses who are out all day for exercise while their owners are at work. On the other hand, if you compete mostly in summer, your feed costs could be almost as high as in

The Truth, the Whole Truth, and Nothing but the Truth!

winter, and you will also have the extra costs incurred in show entries, transportation to show grounds, desirable though perhaps not essential new items of tack and clothing for yourself to bring or keep your turnout up to desired standard and so on.

You may well say: "I don't care how much he costs. He's my hobby and my pride and joy, and I work hard to have him. I'll gladly pay to keep him." I know the feeling, but that's no reason to avoid spending unnecessarily. Most of us have felt the pinch at some time, have wanted a super-quality blanket but could afford only a medium-quality one, have blanched at an emergency vet bill or grumbled at the price of hay. No successful business runs on a "money-is-no-object" basis, and the more careful you are with what money you have, the more you can get for it and do with it.

If you consider that keeping a competition horse at home, where you have no board charges, can easily cost you $8,000 a year if you compete at all seriously, and compare that with, say, roughly half that or less for a weekend hack kept also at home, you can see the desirability of watching every dollar. If those horses are boarded or in rented accommodations, your costs can shoot up considerably.

> **Buy what thou hast no need of, and e'er long thou shalt sell thy necessaries.**

You need to sit down routinely and record every single expense throughout the entire year.

Doling out your money is not stingy; it is sensible. Indeed, it may mean the difference between having enough put aside to afford that emergency vet bill or delaying calling the vet because the thought of the bill frightens you and then ending up with a seriously ill horse on your hands. Apart from the suffering caused to the horse, such a situation will almost surely cost you more in the end than calling the vet in the early stages.

So, then, sit down with a piece of paper and a pen when you have time to concentrate, and do the job properly, writing down absolutely every expense from the past year that you can remember. Even if you have not kept your feed bills, you will have a fairly accurate idea of how much your average bill is for the feedstuffs you buy. You know how much you pay your farrier for a new set or pair of shoes or for a trim. You know how much your rent or board is, if applicable. Also, write down every little item of tack you bought over the year—that flashy new brow band that created a judge's-eye-catching contrast with your horse's coat color, that new bit you tried but discarded and your own clothing, including such seemingly insignificant items as hair nets or thermal insoles for your boots!

List repairs as well, from a major restuffing of your saddle to mending of a tiny rip in your New Zealand rug or restitching of a single stirrup leather. To be fair, you should also list postal expenses for paying bills and sending off show entries, equestrian book and video purchases and magazine subscriptions, instruction and clinic fees, traveling expenses to and from your boarding stable or off-home premises and even those specially purchased tidbits your horse demands. Otherwise, you are not telling yourself the truth.

If you want to do things the accountant's way, you should work out the dollar value of your horse and all his and your equipment, taking into account its depreciation, and determine how much interest you would have earned on that amount of capital in a year in a high-yield certificate of deposit. If your premises are at home, calculate how much less property tax and insurance cost you would have to pay if you had no stables, feed-storage facilities or paddocks, and add that to the calculations.

When you have listed absolutely all your expenses, add them up and divide them by twelve or fifty-two to arrive at the monthly or weekly amount your equestrian activities are costing you. If you haven't fallen over in a faint, you can make things look slightly better by subtracting from that total the amounts of any winnings or earnings you have accrued. Then, to be cruel to yourself, imagine how much interest your yearly expenditure plus the

> **Wealth is not his that has it, but his that enjoys it.**

capital value of horse, etc. would have earned if you had invested it in the aforementioned high-yield account—an interesting evening's doodling—to show just how expensive horses really are to keep!

To be honest, of course, one of the uses of money is to bring pleasure, and if your horse is something you cannot live without, this is money well spent. Looking at it that way, the more you save on expenses, the more pleasure you can get from it! At least, you will be able comfortably to put some by for a critical time in your horsy activities, such as an unexpected illness or accident, instead of operating on a hand-to-mouth basis every week or month. Having worked out the true expenses of keeping a horse might just make you realize how desirable it is to keep a tight rein (no pun intended) on costs.

Your Budget

Budgets are things which none but the most fortunate businesses can run without. Most other operations, from households to private individuals—in other words things which are not normally regarded as businesses—also run on a budget, even though they may not realize it. You have to cut your coat according to your cloth, whatever your circumstances.

A budget is really just a money timetable, and timetables are an excellent way of insuring that, as far as possible, things run according to plan. Schools, for instance, would be chaos without a timetable. So would public transport systems and any business or other operation which runs on an appointment or consulting period/surgery system, such as dentists, doctors, veterinary practices, advisory services and the like.

It will be quite simple to work out a budget for yourself, having done the totting up described in the preceding paragraphs. Even if you have no business experience, you may have heard of something called a cash-flow statement or forecast. This is simply a crystal-ball operation, whereby a business person makes estimates (glorified guesses) of how much money he or she will be spending on a certain item in a certain month. Then, if wise, he or she will make sure that the money needed to pay those expenses is available at the time required, either from what the business earns, from bank loans or from an injection of personal money being put into the business.

> Money, like trains, runs best when kept to a timetable.

The amateur horse owner will need to operate in a very similar way by allocating money regularly from salary or other income to make sure his or her money timetable/budget/cash-flow forecast is running on schedule.

First you will need a large sheet of paper (a legal-size sheet may be adequate or two notebook-size sheets taped together end to

	January		February		March		April		May		June		July		August		September		October		November		December	
	Budget	Actual	Budget	Actual	Budget	Actual	Budget	Actual	Budget	Actual	Budget	Actual	Budget	Actual	Budget	Actual	Budget	Actual	Budget	Actual	Budget	Actual	Budget	Actual
Livery																								
Rent																								
Feed																								
Bedding																								
Farriery																								
Veterinary																								
Instruction																								
Horse box/trailer maintenance																								
Gas/diesel/oil																								
Tack (inc. repairs)																								
Horse clothing																								
Rider clothing																								
Entry fees																								
Postage																								
Premises maintenance																								
Land care and maintenance																								
Hire of facilities (jumps, manege)																								
Subscriptions																								
Registration fees																								
Sundries																								
TOTAL																								

A Basic Budget Form

end). As the accompanying illustration shows, draw a line across the top for the months of the year, a bottom line for totals and as many other lines in between as you have categories, plus a few more for forgotten items or new ones that crop up as you go along.

Next, rule it vertically so that you end up with twenty-six columns for figures and a wider column down the left-hand side for you to name the items the figures relate to, e.g. board, shoeing, veterinary expenses, transport, etc. At the head of the figure columns put "January" over the first two, "February" over the next two and so on to the end of the year. Over the two final columns on the right-hand side put "totals." You now have your empty budget sheet, ready and waiting for your figures.

You have, from your previous calculations, the figures you spent on each category over the previous twelve months, but inflation is still with us, so here you must make a reasoned guess at what inflation is going to be over the forthcoming twelve months. If you think it will be 5 percent, multiply all your individual category totals by that percentage and add that amount to the previous year's costs to give you a probable figure for the forthcoming year.

Do not, however, then divide your estimate equally by twelve to give a monthly figure; some figures will vary according to the season. Your board or rent charge may be the same year round, but transportation costs may not be if, for instance, you don't compete in winter. Here you have to use your common sense, based on last year's actual events (and bills/receipts, if you have kept them) and, within your total, allocate a reasonable amount for that particular expense to each month.

Put your expected figure—your budget or forecast figure—in the left-hand column under each month. Do this for every item, every month. Then total up each month and write in the figure in the relevant space on the "total" line which runs along the bottom of your sheet. Next, add up your categories across the columns and put each category total in the first of the two total columns running down the right-hand side of your sheet.

In the bottom right-hand corner you will have two blank total spaces. Add up all the totals along the bottom line (whatever did we do before home calculators were invented?) and pencil in the figure you get in the left-hand space. Now add up all the totals in the column you have filled in down the right-hand side of the sheet, and see what your calculator says. It should say the same as the figure you have already pencilled in. If it does, it is said to "balance." Assuming it does, ink it over and you have completed your budget.

> **The wise forecaster sees not costs' decline, but bets on bigger bills each year to come.**

You will notice, however, that you have just as many columns left blank as are filled in. These empty columns on the right of your "budget" or "forecast" figures are where you fill in your "actual" monthly expenditures for the categories as you go along. This enables you to see how you are doing as the year progresses. If your actuals are regularly more than your budgets, you've got a problem. Either your sums were wrong in the first place or inflation is significantly more than you expected or your costs have risen quite unexpectedly (perhaps the boarding stable changed hands, and the charges were raised) or your calculator batteries were running down!

At least you can see in black and white what is happening, giving you fair warning that you are going to overspend if things carry on as they are. This can signal you to make economies in other areas or to allocate more money from your income, if you want to avoid getting into trouble.

Should you be fortunate enough to be accumulating a surplus instead of a deficit you may, if you wish (you are the chairman of this particular company, after all), go on a spending spree and buy a new saddle or a luxurious cooler with your monogram on it. On the other hand, if you were intending to buy a new saddle and/or cooler anyway, but omitted to put the relevant cost into your budget, their subsequent purchase could play havoc with your money timetable and you will almost certainly show a deficit at the end of the year.

That is basically how a budget works, and if you have never used one before you will be amazed what a tempering effect it has on your spending urges. It also gives you a self-satisfied glow when you see everything running according to plan, with your actuals very near your budgets. Should your end-of-year forecast totals come within 1 percent of your actual totals, apply to the Office of Budget Management for a job—your country needs you!

Before you dash off to prepare your cash-flow forecast, there is one more thing: It is very wise to set up a "contingency fund" or "emergency fund." As its name implies, this is a reserve fund to fall back on in unexpected, dire circumstances (you have a fall and your saddle tree is broken; your trailer sustains four flat tires due to animal rights activists scattering tacks in the road; a gale whips the roof off your hay shed and, for some strange reason, your insurance policy does not cover it, etc., etc., etc.). This

She who puts aside a little cash for some contingency sleeps easily.

contingency fund can be as large or as small as you like or as your finances permit, but there should be one of some kind. Perhaps an additional ten percent on top of your yearly forecast figure would be adequate and reasonable? Well, maybe 7.5 percent, but something, anyway.

Where to Put Your Money

Having a bank account and the associated record of your deposits and withdrawals and out-payments is by far the simplest way of keeping track of your horse-related expenses. If you take the trouble to fill in all check stubs with the date, the name of the payee (the person you are paying), what the payment was for and the invoice (bill) number, if appropriate, together with the amount, and if you keep a running balance, adding on all amounts you pay in and subtracting what you pay out as you go along in the spaces provided for this on the check stubs, you have a ready-made record always at hand.

Whenever you write out a check you have an instant receipt and proof of payment for the item concerned. Even if you forget to fill in the check stub, your bank can confirm whether or not any check you query has been cashed. Then when your feed supplier keeps sending you nasty letters about an allegedly unpaid bill you can throw unassailable proof in his face.

I find it a good idea to write on the back of the check itself what the payment was for, again adding an invoice number if there is one. Then, if you lose your stubs once the book is empty, you can always refer to the canceled check and the information will be there on the back ready for you. If you want to be really careful, write on the invoice the number of the check with which you paid it. Then it won't take you more than a few seconds to confirm, from the statement of your account which the bank will send you regularly, whether and when payment was made.

Most banks now offer interest, albeit low, on checking accounts but you usually have to keep a minimum amount in the account or in another one with the same bank. Another useful service often offered as a package with an interest-bearing checking account is a small free overdraft. In other words, no service charge or interest is charged on an overdraft of a certain, named amount, say $250. This facility might be extended, for example, to an automatic overdraft of, say, $1,000 on which you pay interest on only the last $750. Since you don't have to ask permission to take advantage of this overdraft offering, you may find it very useful if your income is erratic or you have a lot of unexpected expenses. It can be cheaper than using your credit card, depending on exact conditions. Interest charges begin accruing immediately with an automatic overdraft, excluding the initial free amount if this applies, so if you can be sure you can recoup the amount within the free-credit period offered by your credit card company, you would obviously find it cheaper to use the card rather than the overdraft.

A passbook savings account generally offers higher interest rates than checking accounts, but managing payments and withdrawals without a checkbook is an inconvenience. But any type of account is better than stuffing your money in jam jars around the house or keeping it under the mattress. It will be safe, you will be given a book in which all the transactions on your account are recorded, so again you will know just where your finances stand. And because the money is safely put away, the temptation of dipping into it is largely removed.

Certificates of deposit (CDs) pay more interest than the interest-bearing checking and passbook savings accounts at present, sometimes considerably more if you deposit over a certain amount in them, calculated on a rising scale in increments, usually, of $500 or 1,000. With whatever sort of account you open other than a checking account, find out how quickly you can get at your money. Some tie up your money for months or years, paying you a higher rate of interest the longer you commit it for. If you are happy only with "instant access," i.e. you want to be able to walk into the branch or office and get your money on the spot, make this quite clear when you inquire about the various accounts so that you do not get any nasty shocks later and end up with a sheaf of bills you cannot pay for several weeks or months and a mob of angry creditors. If you get a reputation for late payment, even if it is due to a misunderstanding, you will find services hard to procure in the future. Most banks and savings and loans allow you instant access to your money anyway, but you pay a penalty and lose the interest on the amount you withdraw, which I feel is a minor penalty for remaining in your suppliers' good books.

Having opened your account, of whatever kind, you must steel yourself to pay into it every week or month whatever amount your budget sheet tells you you're going to need that month to keep your horse. If you have a job, your employer may be willing and able to deposit your salary, either all or part of it, as you

> **Interest earned buys more than interest paid.**

> **If you know how to spend less than you get, you have the philosopher's stone.**

prefer, directly into a bank account. If your income is from an investment source, you should again be able to have the money paid directly into an account.

If you have a personal checking account at a bank, it is a simple matter to open a special "horse account" and have a regular automatic transfer made from your personal account to your horse account by means of a standing order—a payment from the personal account into the Horse Account on prearranged dates, such as the first day of every month. However, if your budget shows differing amounts each month and you prefer to stick to the monthly/seasonal variations exactly, a standing order will not do because if you keep changing the amount of your standing order you will soon become unpopular with the bank and may be charged for the service. You will simply have to pay the relevant amounts in yourself, by check from your personal account or just by signing a transfer form at the bank.

If you have budgeted carefully and allowed for a contingency/emergency fund, you should find that, instead of a financial cliffhanger each month, your horse account builds up gradually over the year. This means there will be extra cash in a current account not earning high interest, and you should transfer the surplus into one of the higher interest-bearing accounts mentioned above. Then you won't have to pay for your horse's Lifesavers, sodas or whatever it is he craves out of your carefully put-aside horse money; the interest from your bank or savings and loan will pay for them instead!

How to Avoid Spending Money

Having discussed a suitable home for your money and methods of money management, let's think about ways of not spending it.

If, like many people, you have to keep your horse away from home, your biggest expense will be board charges. This is usually an all-inclusive charge covering rent of stall and grazing, labor for the horse to be looked after and exercised and the costs of his feed and bedding.

In many areas of the country, particularly those near or actually in towns and cities, good boarding stables and services are extremely hard to find. The most popular areas are on the outskirts of the urban areas or just into the rural parts. These areas are reasonably easily accessible for owners and are usually near fair riding facilities (not many owners of boarded horses would be content with riding round and round the same indoor school, riding ring or even in the same few fields all the time), offering commuters or city dwellers a chance to enjoy their horses in the countryside or at least away from the city's noise and fumes. Urban establishments are normally near parks which offer riding facilities.

The boarding-stable proprietor obviously bases his or her charges on the his overhead, and business rates play a large part in this. Owners might reasonably expect to pay more for board in an urban establishment than in a semi-rural one, all else being equal. As discussed in Chapter 1, the best guide to choosing a good establishment is the condition of the horses and ponies already in residence, yet you would, of course, also be far happier if you were at a stable where you liked the proprietor and staff. Although we are currently thinking of how to save money, it might be better to spend a bit extra to be sure of a good place and have the peace of mind this brings, rather than pinch pennies and worry about your horse's welfare all the time.

Cut Back on Board

If, like many people, you do not have much choice as to the actual stable you use, boarding barns being hard to come by in your chosen area, consider ways in which you might be able to pay a little less without compromising on your horse's care. For instance, your stable might charge more for stabling your horse in the main barn with easy access to the indoor arena than in one of the more distant and less deluxe satellite buildings. It is lovely, of course, to have the convenience of being in the main barn, provided the horse is able to watch what is going on in the stable and feel part of things, if that is what he prefers, or conversely he can be quiet and peaceful, if that suits him better. But if the board charge is stretching your bank balance somewhat (or even if it isn't) and there is a stall in the "boondocks," which would do the job just as well for a few dollars a week less, why not have that one instead? Similarly, if your charge includes use of show jumps and cross-country course but you and your horse never jump a stick, why not try to negotiate a reduction in your payment?

This might be construed by some as nit-picking; I prefer to call it avoidance of waste (why pay for something you don't want?) or economizing. It may be that you have to pay a flat fee for everything whether you like it or not, but there is no harm in

> **All things are cheap to the saving, dear to the wasteful.**

> **Paying for impressive facilities never-used buys no benefit for your horse.**

asking. Some stables do charge a flat fee for services offered, but others charge you only for what you actually want. For instance, if your horse is not being turned out to graze for some reason—perhaps because he is ill—you should not be charged for the use of the field during that period. If he is ill and not being exercised, you should not be charged for exercising either. Although the stable proprietor may claim that a sick horse takes up as much time in nursing as a healthy one takes in other respects, this is not normally true. Grooming a healthy horse, for example, takes a good half-hour a day, but no sick horse should be subjected to such a lengthy grooming every day. He would be much better off left in peace and messed with as little as possible, short of being made to feel alone and neglected.

You will be governed largely by the stable's pricing policy, but there are ways of economizing on boarding fees if you think about and discuss with the manager the possibilities of economizing before you move your horse in. If the stable produces an itemized list of services and appropriate charges from which you can pick and choose, by all means take advantage of it. But if not, be sure to find out whether different stables are charged at different rates and exactly what facilities and services are thrown in (e.g. use of riding arenas and jumps, tack cleaning, laundering of blankets, use of horse-walker, etc.) so that you can negotiate terms suitable to your circumstances.

If you do have a choice of stables that would meet your horse-care requirements, it may be worth foregoing the indoor school and/or outdoor ring, the automatic waterer in the stall and the cross-country course you do not need—not to mention the main-stable setting just discussed—and opting for the cheaper, less impressive establishment which will still ensure your horse's well-being and happiness, especially if it is a bit nearer your home and therefore quicker and cheaper to get to.

Economize on Equipment

You will not normally be bothered with equipment, feed and bedding costs and the like in minute detail if you board your horse. However, if you are responsible for these yourself, because your horse is either at home or in a do-it-yourself boarding situation, you will soon become cost conscious and will be on the lookout for ways to reduce expenses in these areas.

It usually pays to get good-quality equipment of whatever sort because of its longer wearing qualities and superior in-use benefits. This applies to tack and clothing as well as to equipment, such as stall-cleaning tools, grooming kits, buckets and so on.

You may consider acquiring certain expensive items, such as tack, harness and New Zealand rugs, secondhand, and this is quite feasible as long as you know what to look for—no cracked, stiff leather or worn, rotten stitching. Secondhand, good-quality equipment and tack is far preferable to brand-new, poorer quality stuff. Used saddles and bridles are often available at tack stores, and if you go to a reputable firm, you should be assured of the safety and good repair of the secondhand tack being offered for sale there.

Other equipment, such as wheelbarrows, feed bins, brooms, shovels, and so on, can often be bought at farm sales, in particular, or occasionally at sales where riding establishments or other agriculture-based enterprises are closing down. The classified advertisements in your local farming press or regional equestrian publication, if you have one, might also reveal bargains in such goods. But don't make the mistake of spending dollars in gasoline or paying heavy transportation charges to get your haul back home. You could end up having spent as much as you would have done if you had bought new nearer home.

If you keep your horse in company with other owners at a do-it-yourself stable and are responsible for finding all your own equipment, there are various ways in which you can save some cash. An excellent scheme I once participated in is for all the owners to join in a "kitty budget," with each owner paying an identical amount per horse to a separate fund each week or month. The kitty bought a communally owned pool of equipment, including stall-cleaning tools, cheap halters for leading to and from the field, a third-hand harrow for the paddocks and so on. (The social aspects of operating like this are discussed in the

> There was never a good knife made out of bad steel.

The wheelbarrow is the most expensive single item of stall-cleaning equipment.

next chapter, but basically it can work very well in practice.)

If there are, say, eight owners in the stable, it is unlikely that all eight will be present and cleaning stalls at exactly the same time, so there is no point in each owner buying a full set of mucking-out tools. Instead, two or three sets could be purchased from the fund. The most expensive item of stall-cleaning equipment is the wheelbarrow, and searching out a secondhand model, even one in need of a handyman's attention, can produce a real savings.

However, a wheelbarrow is not really essential to effective stall maintenance. Polyethylene mucksheets, which are circular in shape with a drawstring round the outside, can be laid outside the stall door and the soiled bedding forked onto them. Then, the drawstring can be pulled tight and the "sack" heaved over your shoulder and hauled off to the manure heap—if you have the strength. An even cheaper alternative is to open out a feed sack—again polyethylene, which seems to have almost universally replaced burlap (paper and plastic are obviously useless for our purpose)—pile the manure on and simply gather up the four corners to contain the soiled stuff. This is not quite so effective and you will probably lose some out of the sides, but it is certainly very economical.

A most useful item of equipment is a manure basket, so that when you are present you can regularly remove droppings and thereby avoid any more soiling of bedding than is absolutely essential. Tack stores and equipment catalogs sell manure baskets, but there is no need to buy one, as you can easily find cheaper or even free substitutes, such as an old household laundry basket. Any sturdy but lightweight container with handles and a wide enough opening for easy pitchfork tipping will do.

The "do-it-yourselfers" kitty fund can also spring for a few communal halters—four being adequate for eight horses and owners. You will all want your own for such things as attending shows, trailering, tying up in the stall and so on, but having a pool of cheap ones takes some of the wear and tear away from your best ones. If any horse has to have a halter left on in the field because he is hard to catch, it is safer to use an old leather one as it will break under strain should the horse get hung up on the fence or catch his hind foot in the halter when scratching his ear. (This can happen even with well-fitting halters.) Nylon halters are cheap but strong and are not, therefore, suitable for field use.

The kitty budget can be regularly boosted by putting into it the money from the sale of the stable's manure, to nurseries or private individuals (or perhaps you might be interested in going into business producing and selling your own mushrooms!).

> **Why buy for yourself when a group can share the cost?**

Buy in Bulk

With the other owners at your stable or other horsepeople in your neighborhood, you are in a position to take advantage of bulk purchase prices of

- bedding,

- feedstuffs,

- professional transport to shows or clinics,

- veterinary supplies, such as deworming medicines,

- professional services, such as annual or six-monthly checkups, tooth work, vaccinations and farriery services.

Vets and farriers are very busy people who do not charge traveling time and expenses for fun. They would rather do several horses on one visit than waste time tripping backwards and forwards, time they could use for other calls. As a commune or cooperative, you split one visit fee between you. Similarly with most professional services, such as freeze marking, custom saddlery work and equine dentistry, it costs less per horse if several horses are done together than if the operator has to make a special visit for one horse.

To enjoy, as an individual, significant savings on feed and bedding, each owner in the stable or community group works out how much hay (or whatever commodity is being purchased) his or her horse will need over a given period; then all the owners' figures are added together and a quotation obtained from a merchant or farmer for that quantity. When the invoice arrives, each owner pays his or her portion of the cost, so buying only what he or she needs but enjoying the lower bulk price.

If your do-it-yourself stable has a manager (probably the owner of the premises), he or she could be delegated to manage the kitty budget and bulk purchase arrangements. If this is not feasible, you will need to elect from among you a responsible individual to take on the job and keep proper, if simple, records of who has paid what and when—but hopefully this shouldn't be too difficult.

Reduce Feed Costs

As well as buying in bulk, there are other ways of economizing on feeding without undercutting your horse's nutritional standard. Remember that many "big name" concentrate mixes are

> **While paying for the name, she forgot the substance.**

more expensive and no better than others made locally or regionally by lesser-known firms. The analysis will be on the bags of all reputable makes, so if you don't understand it (and few of us ordinary mortals do) note down the details and check with your vet or an equine nutritionist on its suitability.

Feed supplements, too, can be very expensive, so check whether there is a cheaper one that would do your job just as well or whether, in fact, you need a supplement at all.

Your horse or pony will, of course, eat more if he feels cold, so do take advantage of the excellent modern range of horse clothing now available to insulate him against cold and wet. If he is stabled, his stall should be well ventilated without there being any gaps between boards or under the door. Many people sweep the bedding away from behind the door to prevent the horse "walking" it out with him but, for warmth, I prefer to actually bank it up there. It protects against drafts and also gives the horse something soft to stand on when he is in.

The less of his coat you clip off, the less he will feel the cold, and therefore the less of his feed he'll use for heating purposes. If you are doing light work it is worth considering a minimal clipping style or even no clip at all. Only horses with very thick, greasy coats

Metal barrels with heavy, fitted lids protect food from rodents, moisture, and even gluttonous horses.

really need a full or hunter clip. Horses with any "blood" in them at all could manage perfectly well in fast work with a blanket clip which protects the vital back and loin areas.

Note, also, that horses' tails were designed by nature to have an insulating and protective function. Full tails look lovely on horses provided they are well kept; they can always be braided for special occasions, and they look much more attractive than pulled tails, to me anyway. The most important point is that the full dock hair protects your horse's vulnerable buttocks region against cold winds. Horses always stand with their tails to the wind, and studies in America with very similar groups of horses kept under identical conditions show that those with pulled tails lost twenty percent more condition during a winter living out than did those with natural full tails. So the moral is obvious.

Protect What You've Paid For

Waste in feeding is also expensive. Galvanized storage bins or hoppers not only keep your feed in good shape but are vermin proof, which sacks are not. Plastic garbage cans make a fair substitute (although determined rats have been known to chew through them), but make sure the lids cannot be knocked off by horses accidentally gaining access to the feed room. Not only

> **Wasted feed feeds only your debt.**

To avoid mold and spoilage, don't buy more than a two-week supply of rolled, cracked, or otherwise milled grain.

might the whole bin go over but horses can become very ill as a result of overeating grain. If several bins or garbage cans of the same height are neatly aligned, a pole can be passed through the handles on all the lids and fastened to the feed room wall or partition in the same way as slip rails are fastened across a gateway—into a holder with a drop-down block of wood to prevent a horse's lifting it out.

Always check with your feed dealers about the recommended storage conditions and "shelf life" of feedstuffs, and do not buy

Hay keeps best in dry, ventilated buildings protected from the weather.

more than you can use in that period as the rest will only "go off" and be wasted. This particularly applies to feed supplements; it is no use buying the large economy size if it will not keep long enough for you to use it up.

If you like feeding individual grains, such as oats or corn, rather than coarse mixes or processed concentrates, don't buy more rolled, cracked or otherwise milled grain than you can feed out in two weeks. These grains, with their protective kernels crushed, are wide open to mold and spoilage and will become unfit to feed if conditions encourage deterioration. Whole grain bought in bulk is not without its problems, as well. Unless stored at the correct temperature and humidity, it may begin to sprout. Few one- or two-horse owners have the appropriate storage facilities to make bulk whole-grain purchases a true savings. Perhaps, however, you can buy moderate quantities direct from the farmer or grain dealer who does have good bulk storage and thereby realize a worthwhile savings.

Hay is subjected to a great deal of abuse in storage. How often do we see open-sided barns full of hay (and straw, for that matter) exposed to all weathers? Rain ruins the outer bales, and a leaky barn roof can quickly ruin the rest. Hay should ideally be kept in dry, well-ventilated buildings protected from the weather. If it has to be kept outside due to lack of storage, it should be kept up off the ground on a platform or pallets or on a tough plastic groundsheet and covered, at least over the top, by a tarpaulin or more plastic. Buying these materials is cheaper than letting the hay mold or rot, which it will readily do in wet weather. Try to stack the hay against a wall or barrier that will protect it from driving rain and the prevailing wind so that your covering is not easily blown away. Tie the cover down, as well (perhaps with a homemade net made of baler twine), or weight it down with old tires.

You can realize savings on even the small pleasures of your horse's life—his carrot or apple treats—by buying in bulk from local producers or distributors, rather than at the grocery store, and then storing them to prevent waste. Root vegetables and apples keep best in cool, dark, airy conditions (a dry basement closet, perhaps), and are better stored without being washed beforehand. Mesh laundry bags or hanging vegetable bins are ideal storage containers. Remember to thoroughly rinse your stored treats to remove dirt and any chemicals before feeding them to your horse, and buy only unbruised, crisp roots or fruits for storage as any which have dark, soft or moldy patches will quickly turn the rest bad, too.

> **She bought in bulk to save a dollar. When she throws it out, she's fit to holler.**

Using feed racks or nets in a shelter keeps the hay dry. Those with a catch tray minimize waste.

Thwart the Wastrel Horse

Waste is difficult to avoid with some horses; they throw their feed all over the place, trample it in the bedding or mud, blow it around and generally do anything but eat it. Apart from ensuring that your horse's teeth are in good condition and that he is properly dewormed (so you are not feeding the worms as well), there are certain things you can do to control his manners at feeding time.

If feeding outdoors, haynets, although a bit time consuming to fill, keep hay under better control than anything else. They can be the cause of serious injury, however, if a pawing horse were to catch a foot in the ropes and be unable to free himself. Cattle racks do a reasonable job but unless they're constructed with no sharp edges or protrusions, they can be a field hazard to horses as well. The most wasteful way to feed hay is simply to toss it on the ground where it can be blown away or trodden into the mud. Feeding in racks or nets in a field shelter, which keeps the hay dry, is the best solution, provided no horse is going to get chased away and forced to go without.

Feeding concentrates outdoors can also be wasteful, unless someone is going to stand and hold each horse's container while he cleans up, which is rather time consuming. Specially designed ground feeders, constructed to deter spillage are available commercially, as are hanging feeders that can be slipped over fence rails. You can even create a no-cost, tip-resistant feeder by ramming a feed tub or bucket into an appropriate size, discarded vehicle tire.

In the stable you have more possibilities for thwarting wasteful eating habits. Again, haynets are an economical way of feeding, but hayracks are good too, especially the "hay-saver" type that makes the horse take small quantities and prevents him pulling the hay all out in a lump and dumping it on the floor. An old-fashioned hay "well" or manger cuts down on waste as horses tend to stand over it and any dropped hay goes back into the well instead of mixing in with the bedding. These wells can easily be constructed by any competent handyman, but ask him to fit a pullout tray on the bottom for easy cleaning. Indeed, the bits and seeds which remain on the bottom can usefully be added to your chop supply.

If your horse is a quiet grain eater, you can feed him from an ordinary bucket or even from a clean sack or piece of sheeting spread on the floor. However, if he scoops his feed out of his bucket or plain manger or knocks over his buckets, install a triangular, corner feeder fitted with bars across the corners to prevent mealtime muzzle movement. Between the restriction of the grain-flinging muzzle and the feeder's inward-turning lip, the grain remains in the container instead of flying out on the floor.

Play the Feed Market for Better Buys

The cheapest time to buy hay and straw is off the field at harvest time, or even before, if you can be certain it will be well made by your supplier. Buying in bulk at this time, even if you have to borrow money from your bank and pay interest on the loan or overdraft, is cheaper than buying the hay in small amounts as you need it, as you could easily be paying 50 or even 100 percent more by spring, particularly in a bad year.

If hay prices are really getting ridiculous in any particular year, there are various alternatives which you can feed and still give your horse a good diet. Quality oat straw, for instance, is more nutritious on its own than poor hay, particularly if the latter is dusty or moldy. You will need to up the protein content of the rest of the diet, but a short consultation with a vet or equine nutritionist will soon sort out a suitable all-round diet. Another

> **Buying a good feeder is cheaper than feeding the floor.**

In a lean hay year, complete ration pellets can be a thrifty supplement, if not an alternative to hay.

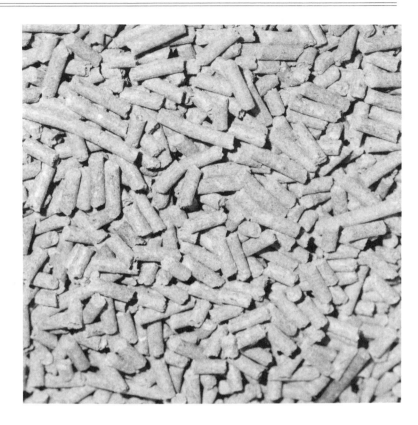

alternative in a lean hay year is to feed commercial roughage products, such as hay cubes or complete-ration pellets. Since these products may have been made in another region or during the previous more-productive season, the price may be cheaper and the nutritional content better than that of the currently available hay. However, your horse may not adapt easily to the processed roughage, and the reduced chew time required for these products may encourage horses to take up wood chewing or other oral vices.

Bran has for the past decade or more been an expensive feed, and it is one that most horses can do very well without. It is overrated as a feed and, indeed, too much in the diet can cause serious imbalance of the calcium-phosphorus ratio, so favoring bone disease. Chopped hay is a safer substitute for adding bulk to feeds and, if you wish to give your horse a mash, soaked sugar beet pulp is acceptable to horses and nutritionally sound.

You should think very carefully before being diverted from a good basic diet, particularly if it has been formulated for you by an expert, just because you have heard of some fancy new feed or additive or supplement which is said to get a horse into tip-top condition and give him bags more energy than he has ever had before. Most of these feeds are expensive and unnecessary. Seek expert advice before using them, and work out carefully what the difference in cost to your budget will be. You may well find that you don't need them and can, in any case, get a cheaper alternative which will do the job just as well.

Bed for Less

Saving on bedding is not simply a case of using the cheapest material you can get. For a start, your horse might need special dust-free bedding, such as shredded paper, because of a respiratory allergy to the dust and spores often found in straw or a skin allergy to the chemicals often found in wood shavings and sawdust. In that case, you must of course use the product which keeps him in the best health. Also, not all materials may be readily available in your area, so you may have to take what you can get.

Assuming you have a choice, obviously the thing to do is compare prices. Start with the one which appears to be the cheapest, then try them all in turn, keeping careful note of what it costs you for each material over an identical period of time under identical conditions.

Naturally, the less bedding you use, the less it will cost you. In this connection, deep-litter bedding, a management system described in more detail in Chapter 7, is certainly the cheapest system you can use. Basically, once the bed is established you need remarkably little material to keep it in good condition.

The enemies of any bed, obviously enough, are droppings and urine. If the horse never dirtied or wet his bed, your problems would be over! It is certainly possible to "house train" equines by teaching them to bang on their doors to be let out when they want to urinate. However, when a working owner's horse is stabled most of the day and there isn't anyone there to let him out, the object of the exercise is defeated and you could end up with a very worried horse!

A horse will normally pass about eight piles of droppings in twenty-four hours, and one of the secrets of successful bedding

> **Trust a thick bed to save you expense;
> a thin one fails both the horse and the floor.**

management, and therefore economy, is to remove them as soon as possible. Again, this is fine if someone is there to pick out stalls fairly regularly but is difficult otherwise.

You do, of course, save on bedding if your horse is out a good deal and, for those not using deep litter, a return to the old cavalry practice of laying bedding in a sheltered spot to dry out, tossing and turning it occasionally, might be considered. This thrifty practice really works only with straw; it would be virtually impossible to manage with shavings, sawdust or shredded paper as they would blow all over the place.

The makers of paper bedding do, however, instruct users to turn and toss the bed to dry it out for reasons of economy. This type of material is recommended to be used on a semi-deep litter basis where it works very well. However, some research done in Britain indicates that, due to its super-absorbent qualities, it is not to be recommended for full deep litter as the amount of urine absorbed into the material can create air-quality problems in stables with even adequate ventilation.

Many working owners make economies of both time and labor on bedding by using semi-deep litter during the week, picking out just the most soiled bedding and saving the full stall cleaning for the weekends. This, too, saves on material provided the bed is adequately managed.

Trouble-Free Flooring

Stable floorings can go a long, way to effect economy of material by helping to keep the bedding dry. Good stable floors achieve this by allowing urine to drain away from the bedding. Old books on management tell us that straw is a drainage bedding, its firm, round stems shedding moisture and the old grooved stable-brick floors draining the urine away to a gutter outside the boxes or behind stalls and thence to an inside or out-side drain. Some stables have a central drain for the purpose right in each stall. I am old enough (just) to remember straw like this and, although like many things it did not work in practice quite as well as in theory, it did drain urine away to a certain extent.

Unfortunately, today's straw is not at all like the old stuff. It is crushed and mangled by harvesting methods and absorbs much

> **To the scientist counting, the horse passes eight piles a day;**
> **to the stall cleaner hauling, it feels like a hundred.**

Straw and wood shavings are inexpensive materials for bedding in stalls.

more urine. Sawdust and shavings are absorbent, too; so is paper, and peat moss (an awful bedding material in my experience) can absorb up to nine times its own weight in moisture. However, it is the lower layers of a bed which naturally get the urine in the end so, at least with straw bedding, drainage flooring will help keep bedding somewhat drier.

A simple earth floor, as used extensively in warm climates, with bedding on top works well in dry areas. In wettish countries like Britain, the stable intended for such a floor should be located on the highest part of the building site to ensure that the natural water table is nowhere near the surface! Local authorities in some areas, depending on their attitude to horses in the environment, might not permit such a flooring and might, whatever system is used, try to insist on an expensive drainage system in

> **To save on bedding, look first to the floor.**

addition unless expert confirmation could be provided that it is not needed.

I kept a horse for a whole winter on an earth floor under straw bedding. His urine simply drained through the earth, there was no residual wet, the bedding stayed quite dry and there was certainly no smell. I used very much less bedding than I normally would on an ordinary floor, and I always like to have a thick, dry, clean bed whenever horses are in as I feel it is kinder to their legs and it encourages them to lie down and rest. Many stall floors in converted buildings originally used for housing other animals or other activities are concrete, which is probably the worst material that could be used. Concrete itself absorbs moisture; it is also cold and hard. Even if grooved in a herringbone pattern ostensibly to take away the urine, this tends not to happen in practice.

The most bedding-saving floors are those that allow urine to drain through them. Probably the best is loose-weave asphalt laid over gravel, over coarser gravel or rubble. The Irish National Stud experimented for some years with various drainage floorings, including concrete slats and perforated concrete slabs over drains, and very much approved of the asphalt floor. They had drains under the gravel, but these are not strictly necessary. Asphalt itself is warm and softer, too, to the horse's feet and legs.

Another drainage flooring is ordinary house bricks, gotten cheap from demolition sites, laid on gravel, or even earth, with a half-inch space all round between bricks. These floors are hard-wearing and allow urine to drain away through the cracks.

Increasingly, stable owners are using stall mats to ease maintenance chores and reduce bedding cost. These rubber-like mats may be solid or perforated. Urine will pool on the solid mats, unless the overlying bedding is quite absorbent or unless there is a central drain, with a perforated cover overlying it, in the stall. The perforated mats allow drainage to the earthen or gravel flooring below, but they can easily become clogged with chaff and other stall wastes. Mats are a great deterrent to the destructive forces of pawing horses and puddling urine and provide a comfortable surface for stabled horses to stand on for long stretches. The initial cash outlay is high, but the cost will be recouped over the long term through reduced floor-maintenance and bedding

---

A paid-for cottage gives snugger shelter than a mortgaged mansion.

costs, not to mention the reduction in the time and labor you put into your daily stall cleaning chores.

Save on Stabling

Economies on stabling can obviously result in large savings. The object of a stable is, of course, to protect the horse from the elements and to keep him clean and handy for us. Although "extras" are desirable, some quite adequate shelters of very basic design—little more than four walls and a roof—can be found accommodating healthy, well-kept horses. The main requirements are good ventilation, a view out, shelter from the elements and dry, safe flooring.

If you are having a horse barn built, there are any number of suppliers of prefabricated timber stables and stalls or firms erecting concrete-block types. Prices vary tremendously depending on structure and your exact requirements. It is almost always cheaper to convert an existing building if something suitable is already located on your property. The main problem with such conversions is that they often have low ceilings which can be dangerous for horses, although many do live safely in them. Even taking into account the fact that plumbing for waterers and electric fittings often have to be moved or have conduits fitted round them to prevent horses interfering with them and that floors almost always have to be changed, usually for reasons of drainage, conversions are still generally cheaper than building new.

Premises with old coach houses and stables attached can be restored and the old stalls made into loose boxes. Larger buildings such as barns, if of sound construction, can be made into stabling by the erection of box stalls. Again, there are a great many suppliers of excellent internal stabling units advertising in equestrian publications.

There is nothing wrong, of course, with using secondhand materials for the sake of economy provided they are strong, and stables do need to be of very strong construction. Corrugated

> **He that builds before he counts the cost
> acts foolishly;
> and he that counts before he builds
> finds that he did not count wisely.**

metal and asbestos sheeting, although often seen, are not strong enough and can easily be dismantled by a determined kicker or by a tied-up horse panicking and pulling back until the structure comes down around his ears. This is false economy in the extreme!

It is also bad practice to make stabling out of heat-conducting materials, such as metal. This makes a stable stiflingly hot in summer and freezing cold in winter. It also encourages a most unhealthy atmosphere inside the stables from which the horse has no escape. Though more expensive to erect, masonry stables are safe, durable, low-maintenance buildings. Construction of double layers of wood with insulation between makes for comfortable stabling. Roofing tiles should have insulating properties or be lined with nonflammable insulating materials (check with your local fire department about suitable materials and also the fire regulations concerning animal housing). Some synthetic stabling materials on the market are both strong and flame-retardant, and new ones are coming out all the time.

Labor costs can be saved if you or someone in your family is good at doing-it-yourself; otherwise, a competent local handyman can be engaged to convert or erect buildings from strong, used materials.

There can surely be nothing as uneconomical as to go to the trouble and expense of erecting stabling or converting some other building only to be told by your local building regulators to pull it down again because you did not have proper building permit or did not apply for change of use of the building. One family in my locality bought a house in a sparsely populated suburb especially because it had an old stable block ripe for renovation and a paddock for their two ponies. The stable had been used as a garage and general storage place for thirty years but, as it had originally been used for housing horses, they thought nothing of putting it back to its proper use. They spent a good deal of money and effort on the restoration, which was tastefully and properly done, moved the ponies in and promptly received notice from the local zoning board to remove them because they did not have permission to keep horses on the premises. They should, apparently, have applied for change of use of the "garage" back to stabling. They put the ponies in a boarding stable, applied for change of use to the building's original purpose and were refused! The house move and renovation had cost them over $12,500, and they still had to board their ponies away from home.

Cut Vet Bills with Clean Air

Anything you can do to improve the stable environment will reduce work and costs in the long run as your horse will be healthier and need less veterinary attention. Stable ventilation is probably the most often overlooked environmental concern. Simply leaving the top of a Dutch door open is quite inadequate, as is also leaving the window open on the same side of the stall as the door. You need facilities to create overhead cross ventilation through eaves-high louvers or simply a removable plank on the wall opposite the door, or, of course, another operable window. Ridge-roof ventilators should be standard equipment on all stables, in my view, so that warm, stale air will be drawn upwards and away.

> **Pay for ventilation, or pay for the vet.**

The most dangerous pollutants in a stable are those arising from decomposing urine and droppings, particularly ammonia, a heavy gas that gathers in the lower part of the stall if there is no draft to remove it. Although floor-level air inlets are often advised in some old and not-so-old books on stable management, I have yet to find a way of providing a floor-level air inlet without also creating a draft. I find the best way to cope is to scatter a commercial stall "sweetener" on the raked floor after cleaning (cat litter, bought in economy-sized sacks, does just as good a job more cheaply) to absorb the gases to a large extent. I also leave the bottom door open whenever possible, such as when the horse is out. You can install a bar, chain or webbing restrainer in the doorway for use when the horse is stabled and keep the full door always open for better air circulation except during cold, blustery conditions. Unfortunately, if your horse is the sort who puts his legs everywhere including over the bar, chain or whatever, you cannot do this. In such cases, you might like to fit a cage-type lower inner door.

Save with Sheds

While on the subject of stabling, it is as well to consider whether in fact you need it at all. A stall is certainly an advantage, particularly if you want to keep a horse in for convenience or if he is sick and needs, indeed probably wishes, to be isolated. But there are other cheaper methods of accommodating horses which are also more appropriate to their natural ways.

A method mentioned in Chapter 1 is yarding, which I feel could be made much more use of for better management of

space, time and labor. Many a small area could usefully have a
run-in shed erected and kept bedded on deep litter and the open
fenced-in area in front of it floored with some suitable material
such as a mixture of peat and sand, wood chips or used bedding
minus droppings. A shed for two loose horses, for example,
should be a minimum size of sixteen feet by twelve feet. It does
not need any special flooring, although it is nice to keep it bedded
on deep litter as mentioned, the bedding being put directly on
the earth. Such a shed, having no expensive fittings such as
windows or doors or a partition to separate the two horses, is
considerably cheaper than two stalls. The horses have each other
for close company, and they have the freedom to be outside in the
attached enclosure or under cover in the shed as they wish.

The shed—which should, as discussed, be strongly built—can
have a long hayrack down the back wall or rings for haynets. In
inclement weather, the horses may need to be blanketed in New
Zealand rugs if they choose to spend most of their time in the
unprotected portion of the yard.

This method, of course, is very similar to keeping horses out in
a grass paddock with a field shelter, except that stabled horses do
not get anything like as dirty as their field-kept counterparts, the
flooring material, unlike mud, being easily brushed off.

On the continent of Europe, it is common practice for large
herds of breeding stock (not necessarily quiet-natured, cold-
blooded types of horses but spirited competition breeds and
bloodstock) to be out during the day and brought into large,
deep-litter-bedded barns at night rather than individually stabled.
Many stud farms run on such lines would not exist if they had to
spend the money and labor involved in stabling their animals in
a more conventional way.

Apart from the great savings in time and money, such accommodation arrangements go down very well with the horses, who
have a much more natural life associating closely and freely with
their own kind. They learn herd manners and are used to being
disciplined by their elders and superiors in the herd, and therefore they take to human discipline much more kindly than
animals who have been kept in a more unnatural way. These
animals are communally fed their concentrates and hay in continuous mangers and hay holders running round the walls of the
building.

When it comes to removing droppings, this is of course a
chore, but one much more quickly completed than doing the
equivalent number of box stalls.

> **Shed-raised horses take half the work, half the cost, and half the discipline.**

Hired Help: Who Needs It?

The only way to save money on paid labor is, obviously, not to employ it! This of course means that you have to do the work yourself, get a member of your family to do it or take turns with other owners in a communal stable to help each other out. This topic is dealt with in the next chapter.

There are various mechanical means of avoiding the use of paid labor, such as the increasingly popular horse-walkers, horse vacuum cleaners and heat lamps in grooming stalls to dry off wet horses. There are simple means of reducing labor needs, such as riding one horse and leading another (ponying) and so exercising two horses (or even three if you have one on each side, your horses are very well behaved and you have adequate exercise facilities to accommodate the bunch of you safely) in the time it normally takes to do only one. Turning animals out saves some exercising but doesn't really maintain fitness.

The mechanical methods obviously involve the expenditure of money on buying the equipment, but they save money on paid labor in the long run. If paid labor is out of the question anyway, they save work for you or enable you to do more horses and to get jobs done more quickly than you otherwise would. Time saving and money saving are very closely linked in many areas. If your budget can manage the initial outlay, it may be worth "spoiling" yourself with a laborsaving piece of equipment.

Do Away with Shoes

Along with feeding, stabling and labor, shoeing is a significantly expensive item in horse management, and it is one that often comes as a shock to new horse owners. A horse doing two hours' work a day, much of it on roads or rocky going, will surely wear out a set of shoes in six weeks and maybe sooner if the road surface is rough tar and chips rather than a smooth asphalt one.

It is often thought that using heavier shoes will give longer wear, but in fact this is not so. Using heavy rather than medium-weight shoes simply causes the feet to be brought down on the road harder, creating more wear, in fact, on the shoe and more concussion on the foot and leg. Medium-weight shoes are the choice of most people for riding and lightweight driving horses doing road work, and such horses can cope with that weight easily without having their action affected.

If you can reduce wear on a set of shoes, they can be reset for a second go-round, saving you a few dollars on the farrier bill.

Well-maintained hooves are essential to the health of any horse. If the foot conformation and quality of horn are good, there is no reason why the horse should not go unshod.

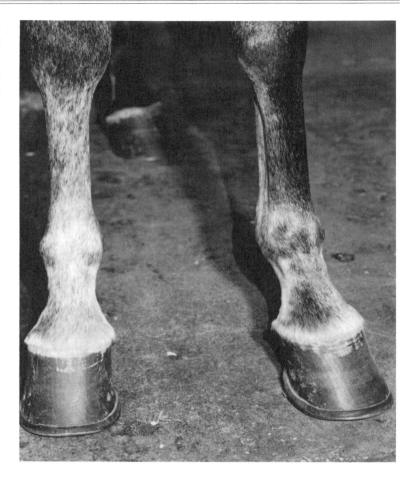

Apart from using soft surfaces such as tracks and road shoulders whenever possible, another method of reducing wear is to get your farrier to weld into the toes and heels or any areas which the horse wears unevenly, some hardener, such as borium. Make sure that whatever hardener the farrier uses wears rough, not smooth, to help prevent slipping.

Perhaps your horse or pony doesn't need to be shod at all for the work you ask him to do. Having him go barefooted could save you several hundred dollars annually. If your horse's work is mainly on soft surfaces or, for limited distances, hard, smooth roads, and if his foot conformation and quality of horn are good and he is on a balanced diet which will help maintain the horn quality, there is no reason why he should not go unshod. (This suggestion is discussed further in Chapter 7.)

To carry the cost-cutting measures even further, you may also trim your horse's hooves yourself, provided you understand how

> Hard work
> and poor hooves
> are the only
> sure call
> for the shoer.

the foot should be balanced and provided your horse does not have any exaggerated faulty action to create grossly uneven wear. Learning to trim and maintain your horse's feet is not that difficult, and if you cannot find a farrier who will show you how, the study of a good book on farriery, such as *Shoeing Right* by David Krolick (Breakthrough), plus common sense and practice will enable you to do a competent job. I know of several people who have to do their own trimming work because the services of a good farrier can't be gotten in their area. Again, you will have to invest perhaps $100 in buying the equipment—nippers, hoof knife, rasp with handle and sharpening tools—but you'll soon recover that amount from saved farrier visits.

Travel for Less

Transporting your horse to events of various kinds can be a considerable expense. If you are doing a lot of traveling, it is obviously very much more convenient to have your own transport than to have to rely on others and much cheaper than having constant transporter's bills to pay. Obviously, a horse van needs to be licensed and insured and is also another vehicle which needs maintaining, but it does score over a trailer in comfort, ride and safety. If, however, you're the typical one- or two-horse pleasure owner, you can hardly justify the purchase of a horse van. Even a trailer, requiring a powerful pulling vehicle and extra insurance and licensing costs, may be far more of a drain than your budget can bear.

> **An unsafe rig is never a cheap way to travel.**

Clubbing together with friends for contracted transport is, of course, fairly economical, although if not enough of you wish to go to a particular event to fill the only van the contractor has available, it could prove more expensive than you had bargained for. Do not, in pursuit of excessive economy, be tempted to put up with an unsafe vehicle, either as regards its road worthiness, its driver or the comfort and safety of the animals traveling in it.

If you "hitch a ride" to an event in a friend's transport, be sure there is no question of "hire and reward," i.e. that you do not pay him or her for taking you, or you could find that whatever vehicle insurance coverage your friend has is negated. (A contribution towards gasoline, however, is another matter.) This whole business of insurance regarding "amateur" horse transportation is a very grey area and, as you will doubtless want some compensation from somebody if your horse is injured during transportation, you would be well advised to check on your own insurance and check with your friend before taking the plunge.

Consider Insurance Costs

It has to be said that if an insurance company can avoid paying out on a claim, then it will surely do so. Insurance companies are in business to make money and will hang on to it like any successful business if they possibly can. Make quite sure you fully understand the terms of any horse-related policies you already have or may considering buying. This is no easy matter, even with a basic policy, so do not hesitate to get confirmation from the company *in writing* of any point about which you are uncertain. Discuss the matter with a lawyer if you feel you are being confused or misled by the company on any point not answered clearly or if they refuse to put an explanation in black and white.

Insuring your horse is sometimes a dicey business. Again, there are many, many complaints about insurance companies finding ways of not paying out on claims, particularly for loss of use when it seems that their vet invariably disagrees with yours! There have been cases reported in the press where a horse was kept suffering unnecessarily because the insurance company insisted on a vet of its choice traveling to see the animal and refusing to take the opinion of policyholder's veterinarian as satisfactory in cases where euthanasia was recommended. Conversely, animals have been put down due to accident or sudden severe illness without the policyholder's being able to contact the insurance company, usually on a weekend or during a holiday, to advise them of the situation. These policyholders have later been denied their payout because of this. I and several people I know have suffered at the hands of insurance companies and, because of our experiences, now feel that mortality insurance is not worth the premiums paid.

> A horse has two values: what it costs to insure him and what he's worth when there's a claim.

Even with medical and loss-of-use coverage, there can be points to watch with some companies. If you make a claim for, say, a sprained tendon, you could find that the company excludes all future coverage for disorders in that leg. If the horse once has a cough, which you claim for veterinary attention, you may never again get coverage for a respiratory disorder of any kind. Even if you can get coverage, the premium could be raised considerably because of these prior claims.

So, the only advice I can give on equine insurance—which is backed up by experience—is that coverage for death or loss of use of your horse is so expensive and so uncertain that it is not worth the expenditure. Cover for veterinary fees is well worthwhile, but before you sign, check up on what will happen to future claims regarding related disorders and get a satisfactory explanation in writing.

You may wish to check on the pros and cons of insuring your tack against theft or damage and your horse against theft. There are various offers available from the many insurance companies involved in this field, and I feel the best plan is to get a few personal recommendations from friends, colleagues and other contacts, asking specifically about particular companies' records on paying out and whether there was a great deal of hassle involved in the process. Most companies will give a significant discount for security-marked tack or a freeze-marked horse. As regards the latter, many people feel it is not worthwhile insuring a marked horse as statistics show that the chances of the horse being stolen and not recovered, as compared to an unmarked horse, are very slim, but this is a matter for personal choice.

Cash-Saving Tips

• Feed hay in the field so that it cannot be trampled in the mud or blown away; feed concentrates in tip-proof containers or hold the bucket of a messy feeder to prevent waste.

• It's cheaper to keep your horse at a "commune"-type stable where you take turns doing the chores and help each other out, than to pay board or labor fees because you haven't time to make two or more daily trips to the stable.

• Always buy in bulk when you can, maybe with friends, as it is cheaper than buying in smaller quantities.

• Be stingy with the stable electricity. Although lights are a good security measure, and horses do not like pitch darkness, keep levels very low if you are leaving them on all night. Sensor-operated security lights are very bright but come on only when the beam is activated.

• Try making your own haynets out of binder twine.

• Run a horsey yard sale or flea market for neighboring horse owners. As well as getting cash for your unwanted bits and pieces, you could buy some bargains from other sellers.

• Buy the best quality you can afford of everything as it will last much longer.

• But don't pay through the nose for fancy packaged feeds and supplements when unadvertised, local products offer adequate nutrition.

• A thick bed is more economical than a thin one and does its job better.

• Don't begrudge the cost of identity-coding your horse. It's cheaper and less painful than replacing a stolen horse.

• Effective parasite control is one of the best methods of saving money on feed, even taking into account the cost of the dewormers.

• Do keep your feeds in moisture- and vermin-proof containers to avoid waste and contamination. Do use an old fridge for storing perishable feeds such as molasses feeds, soaked/soaking sugar-beet pulp and so on.

• Keep your insurance premiums up to date so that previous ones are not wasted should you make a claim two days after yours has run out!

• Keep vaccinations up to date, too; a debilitating or inconvenient illness is considerably more expensive than timely booster shots.

• If you want to pack some extra energy into your horse's ration at a low cost, try adding store-brand corn oil, bought in bulk containers from a "warehouse" grocery, to his concentrate.

• Disposable diapers are good for wrapping legs or feet that are being poulticed.

• Make feed measures/scoops by cutting the bottoms off various size plastic drink bottles or jugs and stick on labels stating how much, by weight, of each food they hold.

• Substitute baby oil for the more expensive branded show-coat conditioners, but don't overdo it with the oil or you'll have an oily mess.

• Get together with neighboring horse owners or the other boarders in your stable to coordinate the farrier's and vet's visits (for example, for annual health/vaccination procedures) on the same day to save on call fees.

• Get your farrier to weld hardening materials into the most-worn parts of your horse's shoes to prolong their useful lives.

• Borrow from friends rather than buy if you need horse-care or stable-maintenance items only occasionally. But be sure to return them promptly and also reciprocate when asked!

• Learn to do basic tack and clothing repairs and adaptations yourself rather than buying new all the time. When buying secondhand blankets and other items that will contact your horse, always disinfect them before use and preferably buy from a source where you know the animals are healthy.

• Find a saddler or harness maker to adapt items of tack, such as making a running martingale into a standing one or adapting a cavesson noseband to become a flash, rather than buying new. For instance, you can create a useful bitless bridle our of a sturdy, strengthened drop noseband and a pair of reins.

• Buy good quality, guaranteed secondhand tack from a reputable tack dealer than new, and have it altered to fit your horse, if need be.

• Think before you buy anything, asking yourself what you can manage without rather than what you can do with!

• Save baling twine and the thread from the tops of feed sacks. They come in useful for all sorts of things from making haynets and macrame halters to doing emergency repairs on fences and horse clothing.

• Don't spend money on expensive items that sound good in advertisements, unless you are certain you need them; this goes for everything from feed supplements to saddles.

• Weigh out feeds accurately so you'll feed correctly. Feeding too much is expensive, wasteful and potentially harmful to your horse.

• Don't buy more perishable feed—such as grains, particularly sweet feeds heavy with molasses and processed concentrates— than you can use within a safe period, as it will go "bad" and be wasted.

• Don't keep hay where it is exposed to the weather, which will leach out nutrients and cause mold to develop.

• Well-cared-for grass is far cheaper than bought feeds.

• Buy blankets in household-goods sales or at charity shops where they are cheaper than "proper" horse blankets. Never mind the colors!

• Do you really need a proper grooming caddie? Instead, use a water bucket to keep your grooming equipment together.

• Buy secondhand wood for fence repairs and jumps.

• House-train your horse, and save on stall-cleaning time and bedding costs! By training your horse to associate, say, a particular low whistling sound with urinating, you can get him to urinate more or less on command outside the stall or into a bucket with a little bedding in the bottom (to avoid the noise and splash, which horses hate). Train him to do his business outside or into the bucket when you return from a ride or bring him in from the field. And remember, many horses urinate when you put down new bedding, so be ready with the bucket.

4

A Little Help
from Your Friends

Anyone who undertakes the care of a horse bears a considerable responsibility not only for his conduct but, directly and indirectly, for his welfare, too. People mistreating animals, whether their own or other people's, can, under the law, be prosecuted, fined, and banned from keeping them for specified periods.

Horse owners who delegate the care of their horses to others are still responsible for the animal's well-being. It is up to them to supervise and see that those other people are, in fact, properly carrying out their duties in relation to the horse's care. Horse owners who look after their horses singlehandedly obviously have total responsibility; even if they fall ill, the horse still has to be cared for, and in such circumstances it is up to them to obtain other help to see to the horse.

This often raises a big problem for those keeping horses either at home or in other accommodation with no other help at all. Not only are they tied down as regards their daily routine, but life can become very difficult if they are incapacitated by illness or injury, even for a short time. There is a great deal to be said for independence, but just as much for being part of a group, even a small one, of like-minded people who work together to help each other out, either just during emergencies or as a matter of course.

> A true friend is the best possession.

Sharing the Homeplace

If you do want to keep your horse at home—for many people having their horse outside the back door, as it were, is the only way they will be really happy about keeping a horse at all—and there is no other member of the family competent to help or in any way involved with your horsey activities, why not consider providing free stabling, grazing and part-time care to one or two other animals in return for companionship for your horse and help from their owners, either on a regular basis or at times specified by you? These owners would be responsible for all their own feed, bedding, shoeing, veterinary and other maintenance expenses but would simply not pay for their stabling and grazing or for the occasional labor you put into their horses. In return, they would help with your horse or horses according to a mutually acceptable agreement.

Such an arrangement can work extremely well for all parties concerned provided you all get along together. Boarding-stable proprietors are well used to being nice to people they don't particularly like! They are in business for money, and although they may prefer to work on a friendly basis with their clients, it is

> Several owners of a single mind
> make shared duties come out fine.

not essential to them. Of course, any owners who are a real pain in the neck or are totally unreasonable in their demands or behavior can be told to take their unwelcome patronage elsewhere.

When you are considering having other people and horses on your own private premises, not for business but for a mutually beneficial, friendly, working relationship, you naturally do not want people around whose ideas of horsemastership differ drastically from your own, whom you do not like or trust or simply can't talk to. "Interviewing" a horse and owner for such a scheme, then, is rather like choosing a friend and an employee in one.

Not only do you have to like both horses and owners reasonably well, you must also get straight between you exactly how the horses are going to be cared for. If the other owners' principles differ greatly from yours, you will not be happy having to treat their horses in a manner with which you disagree, and you are also going to be worried that they will not carry out your wishes and systems in your absence, no matter what assurances they give. A straightforward, honest discussion should, therefore, take place before any promises are made. Be particularly careful to clarify the following aspects of the arrangement:

- what amount of work they will be expected to do in exchange for their free stabling, grazing and part-time care (the provision of which could save them in the region of at least $50 a week at current rates),

- who will be responsible for the maintenance of the stable,

- where you draw the line between reasonable wear and tear and willful damage on the part of their horses,

- what the preventive health-care program will be.

> **The rotten apple spoils his companion.**

It should be stressed that their horses will have to be dewormed at the same time and with the same product (drug), as yours for the sake of keeping your pasture "clean." It takes only one infested horse to infect a paddock and give the other horses on it a continuous worm burden, no matter how carefully they themselves are dewormed, so everyone must be in agreement on this important point. Similarly with vaccinations: It is pointless for some horses to be protected from influenza and rhinopneumonitis if one unimmunized horse falls victim to every epidemic going around and brings the viruses home. Vaccinations give a level of protection, not a guaranteed immunity. If infection is at a high level in the stable because one particular horse has a bad case of flu, even the vaccinated horses might also succumb to mild cases of it.

Having straightened out everything of this nature and found, either through the grapevine or from advertising locally, people and horses you feel you can work with and get along with reasonably well (and vice versa), you may discover that you actually prefer having someone else around to ease your workload a bit and to socialize with, particularly if you are a sociable type of person. If gone into sensibly, such arrangements can work very well for all concerned.

Do-It-Yourself Board This type of arrangement is becoming more and more popular with owners as a means of keeping costs down. Like any other system, it has advantages and disadvantages. The best approach is to use a stable with an official manager who will oversee owners without their feeling as though their business is being meddled with by a person with no right to meddle, as would be the case in a managerless barn. Owners can still do their horses according to their own principles, but any cases of actual neglect or mistreatment can be dealt with. The offending party will, if inexperienced, have matters explained so that he or she knows better in future, while those who refuse to improve will be "sacked," perhaps with an accompanying report to an animal-welfare organization, too, in bad enough cases.

Such managed self-care situations are often found as part of riding schools or boarding centers proper. Particularly in areas where full board is hard to obtain or where a riding school does not want to be particularly bothered with providing normal boarding setups, do-it-yourself arrangements can provide good revenue for the stable proprietor. Boarding of any kind brings in regular income year round and makes up for the sometimes erratic income provided by the riding school part of the business, which may be prone to seasonal fluctuations, particularly if it has no indoor arena.

Other types of do-it-yourself boarding accommodation may be found in various premises which are simply available for rent

> **Better to keep your horse a dream
> than find his keep become a nightmare.**

with no formal supervision of any kind, such as defunct riding schools or other horse businesses, old farm buildings and private premises whose owners simply wish to get a little (or sometimes significant) extra income without having any work involved. Such arrangements can create problems with less-than-responsible owners neglecting their animals. Unlike a managed yard, where the reputation of the entire establishment will matter to the manager, unsupervised stables have no one in charge to care about this sort of thing. The other owners will have no one to report problems to and may end up looking after their own horses in an unpleasant, slapdash atmosphere with which they will not be happy.

A major problem arises in any kind of rented facility or boarding arrangement where the premises have no housing and so have no one there overnight or even, sometimes, during the day. This leaves the horses wide open to theft and abuse, and it is a very poor way indeed to keep an animal. To leave horses alone and not checked on for many hours or even to leave them out of earshot should any horse start thrashing about with colic or some other painful disorder is extremely poor horsemastership. I personally feel it would be better not to own a horse at all than to keep one under such circumstances, as it is grossly unfair to the animal.

The advantages of having help available have been discussed, and I feel there is everything to be gained by all the owners in a do-it-yourself boarding establishment, managed or not, getting together and working out ways in which they can all help each other, not only in emergencies but on a regular daily basis to ease each other's burdens.

Why not call an informal meeting, either in the stable or at someone's house and put forward your ideas of how you could all help each other? If your barn has a manager, she (it usually is a "she") should certainly be invited, as she will be the linchpin of the operation, not actually being involved with the work, except in a genuine emergency, but seeing that messages reach the right people and that each horse is properly cared for.

In the north of England there is a saying that "there's nowt so queer as folk," and it's very true. To make any "commune" type of arrangement work, you all have to be reasonable people, individuals with, most likely, your own ideas of horse management and varying standards, but still able to work with your colleagues for the mutual good. Your common goals would be

A Mutual Cooperation Society

- to ensure that all the horses and ponies in the stable are well cared for,

- to help all participants enjoy savings through cooperative efforts and group purchasing (as detailed in chapter 3),

- to save each other time by helping out on a regular basis as well as in emergencies.

Any horse needs attending to at least twice in twenty-four hours. This involves two trips, two lots of gasoline, two lots of commuting time and two lots of chores for each owner to perform, but if friends/associates get together and agree (even just two friends working together) that one does the horses in the morning and the other at night, think how much easier your day will be.

Imagine a do-it-yourself stable—purely imaginary, I stress comprised of the following people, with their differing time availabilities and work hours:

- a young secretary whose job is largely nine to five but who works "flextime" on occasion;

- a hospital doctor who works long but erratic hours and who is often at the stable at "peculiar" times;

- a factory worker who works irregular shifts on a regular basis (i.e. three day shifts, then three afternoon shifts and finally three night shifts, followed by three or four days off);

- a retail clerk who works mainly nine to five-thirty but all day most Saturdays, with two half-days off (not always the same two) during the week;

- a minister who never stops by on Sundays but is often found at the stable during the day on weekdays and Saturdays;

- two teenagers who attend a nearby school and care for their ponies morning and late afternoon, Monday to Friday, and, of course, nearly all weekend;

- a free-lance riding instructor who keeps her horse at the stable, where she can generally be found when not out on teaching appointments.

> **Many hands make light work.**

The stable also has a manager, who takes messages and generally oversees operations to make sure every animal is properly looked after.

A rotation of duties has been drawn up, by mutual discussion and agreement, among this diverse group of horse owners and is written on a blackboard in the tack room. Those with irregular working hours advise in advance when they will be available. In every case, when one owner's allocated jobs cannot be fulfilled because of his or her absence, someone else takes over.

The secretary's salary is quite low, but instead of paying stall rent she helps the stable proprietor with correspondence on a regular basis. She can arrive at her job at 10 A.M. on certain days, provided that she makes the time up at some point by staying until 6 P.M. Since the two teenagers come to the stable straight from school and can be there to see to her horse at 4.30 P.M., the secretary cares for their horses in the mornings of her "late" days in exchange for their looking after hers on those afternoons.

The retail clerk and the instructor are both present early each

Cooperation in the care of your horse and its quarters can ease the chores and make handling more pleasurable.

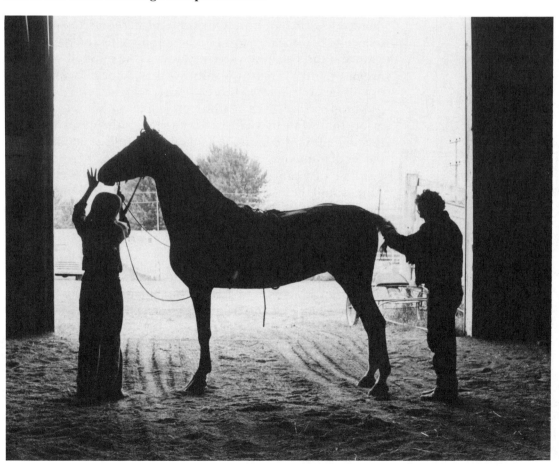

day and see to the animals whose owners are not coming that morning, feeding and turning out according to the other owners' instructions for the day as noted in the "master diary" in the tack room (see Chapter 6).

On her afternoons off, the clerk often exercises another's horse as well as her own, in exchange for their exercising hers on a Saturday when she cannot normally come. The instructor is sometimes away for several days taking courses and clinics, but repays the others for looking after her horse during these times by giving them free lessons and help with schooling problems.

The stable manager keeps the blackboard and master diary up to date by writing in owners' telephone messages and, on the rare occasions when no one at all can be in the stable at a certain time, will feed, water, pick out the stalls and turn out or bring horses in from the field. If her duties become significant, the owners pay for them, in addition to their rent, out of their kitty budget.

I once kept a horse in a do-it-yourself arrangement without an official manager. The stable was owned by an elderly but fairly active lady who would always help by throwing hay over doors and filling buckets from a hose. Our kitty budget regularly paid for the services of a free-lance groom when none of us could get to the yard, and the system worked very well, as the owner lived on the premises and we had two shift workers among us who could usually be present when those working regular hours could not.

As you can see, then, a group of people can work together to insure that, while they still have time to enjoy their own horses, all the animals in the barn are looked after at least adequately by means of mutual cooperation, a flexible rotation of responsibilities, fair play and organization. They all know each other's animals and their foibles well and take an interest in them and so have gained a wider experience of horses and horsemastership than would be the case if they restricted their activities to just one animal, their own.

You really need a stable full of sensible, mature people to make things work. However, children often keep their ponies under such arrangements, and this can be valuable training for them, building character and instilling responsibility.

> **Diligence is the mother of good luck.**

> **Your helper is only as good as the instructions given.**

Whenever other people are involved, it is essential to leave clear and precise details of what your horse should eat.

If you keep your horse at home and do not want, or haven't room for, other people's horses on the premises, you may well be able to rope in at least one member of your family to help while you are at work or away from home. If not, you may be able to book the occasional services of a free-lance groom—be it a professional who works in a large establishment up the road and is willing to help you out before and after her regular duties or an eager Pony Clubber or 4-Her in the neighborhood who would love to earn both the extra money and the experience caring for her favorite animals.

Feed Charts

Probably the single aspect of management most likely to cause problems when horses are being looked after by people other than their owners is feeding. Even though you know your horse's diet inside out, it is essential, where others are involved, to leave clear and precise details of what he should have for each feed, either in a book, on a chart pinned on the wall or on a communal blackboard used for everyone in the stable. Put down the exact details of scheduling and measurement, referring to the weight of the portions rather than simply saying "a scoop of sweet feed" or "a spoon of supplement." Horses have very delicate digestive systems and will not tolerate too many irregularities in feeding, so write it down and make sure substitute feeders have the scales and containers handy to follow your instructions to the letter.

5

Time for Everything

We all have the same amount of time—twenty-four hours in each day-night cycle—yet how often do we hear the complaint: "I haven't got time to do that"? Of course, those bemoaners mean they have too much else to do, but I wonder if they have ever thought seriously not only about how much they commit themselves to but how they do the things they do anyway.

We all have the same amount of time—24 hours in each day-night cycle.

> **Dost thou love life?**
> **Then do not**
> **squander time,**
> **for that's the stuff**
> **life is made of.**

If you constantly feel pressured, if you find it hard to concentrate on what you are doing at this minute and are constantly thinking about what you have to do next, tomorrow, next week or next month, if you get bad tempered easily, even with those you love, if you frequently feel tired, not just healthily, physically tired but draggingly weary, and if you find that you do not seem to get much real enjoyment out of life, not even out of your horse whom you are supposedly keeping for fun—the chances are you are either genuinely doing too much or are not doing what you do do efficiently.

Setting Priorities

The subject of "time management" has become big business in the business world. Large and small companies spend many hundreds, even thousands, of dollars each year sending their key managers to expensive but usually worthwhile time-management courses. There are umpteen good books on time management, all giving a slightly different view of the subject but all agreeing on one key principle: to manage your time effectively you have to get your priorities right.

Setting and judging priorities is the most valuable lesson you can learn from either a course or a book. You must evaluate your tasks accurately so that you are sure which are the most important (not necessarily which are the most urgent, because you'll have to do those anyway). Then write them down as if you were giving someone a list of things to do.

You may think: "What's the point of that? I don't need to write things down. I know what I've got to do—too much!" You will find, however, that if you make a habit of writing yourself what is commonly called a "To-Do List," it will crystalize everything wonderfully for you. It will act as a constant "conscience," and you will get a super feeling of smugness and self-satisfaction when you look at your list of tasks at the end of the day, all crossed off with everything done. There is no need to write every little detail on the list, but you will find it beneficial to extend it to all areas of your life—horse, home, work/business, social—as this gives you a clear picture of the whole of your life's activities, and you can see if any one aspect is taking a disproportionate precedence over the others.

Many time managers recommend that you keep a time log for a week so that you can see what you really spend most of your time doing. It is easy to think you spend more time on one task than you actually do. It is just as easy to overlook how much time you spend reading the newspaper or sitting looking at your in-tray or out of the window wondering if anyone has brought in your horse or at the basket of ironing that you have to do or at the pile of correspondence you never seem to catch up with. In fact, wondering how on earth you are ever going to get everything done is just about the worst way to spend your time, because during that time you are doing precisely nothing—and that is a complete waste of time. It's not even an enjoyable nothing like dreaming what you'd do if you won a million dollars in the lottery. It is an aggravating, depressing kind of nothing.

So stop wondering how you are going to get everything done. There is only one way to get anything done—and that is to get on with it!

> **You may delay, but time will not.**

Fortunately for horse owners, a vital key to time management—setting priorities—is easy, at least as regards the horse-oriented tasks. You simply put the horse first. Make a list of absolutely every single job, big or small, you have to do in relation to your horse, and then divide them into "A" jobs and "B" jobs. The "A" jobs are those which directly affect your horse and the "B" jobs are those which are connected with his care but which do not directly affect his welfare.

The A List and the B List

> **Let your horse decide the most important jobs you do.**

Put yourself in your horse's position to help you prioritize the jobs you have listed. Just imagine what he would care about. He would care about

- getting his food,

- having clean water to drink,

- leaving his stall and stretching his legs,

- having somewhere away from his own excreta to stand and lie down,

- having his blankets or other "clothing" made comfortable.

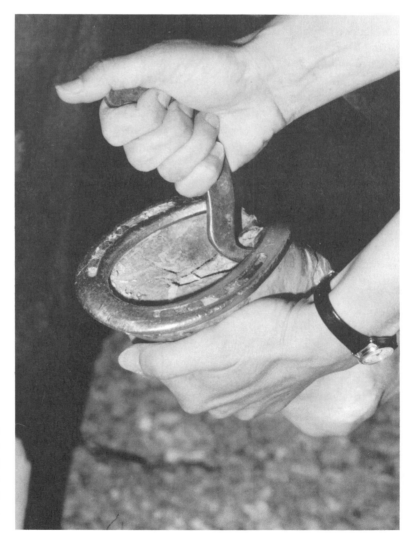

Taking care of your horse's feet should be a priority during your "horse time." It is vitally important for the animal's welfare that its feet be picked and shoes checked twice daily.

On the other hand, he wouldn't care at all about straw blowing about the yard, about peeling paint, about the untidy tack room or about the sprawling manure heap.

The following is a short list of what I consider to be "A" jobs, those which should take priority during your "horse time" and which are all very important because they directly affect the horse:

- feeding and watering
- stall cleaning
- adjusting/changing blankets
- cleaning feed and water containers
- maintaining the stable for the horse's safety and health
- exercising
- picking out feet, cleaning eyes, nose and dock
- cleaning the underside of tack, which touches the horse
- maintaining fencing so the horse can be turned out safely

Now here is a list of (in my book) "B" jobs which, although important, do not directly affect the horse himself and so should not take priority over "A" jobs:

- full grooming (in between "A" and "B"!)
- sweeping/raking the stable yard
- stacking feed/hay/bedding
- painting the woodwork
- full tack cleaning
- tidying the tack room
- cleaning tools
- tending the manure heap

If some readers are horror-stricken by my list, I should stress that this book is intended for people who are keeping horses on a very limited time budget. Anyone with a job to do, a business to run or a young family to look after has limited time. It is quite possible for one horse to take up a whole working day if we let him. Work really does expand to fill the time available for its completion (I can't remember who said that, but it's very true) but I prefer to turn things around and make the work diminish so that I spend more of my valuable time doing the things I really want to do, like riding my horse or just being with him, rather than sweeping the stable yard or cleaning tack, straightening out drawers or cleaning the windows.

I have a particular aversion to spending my time looking after a manure heap. I cringe every time I hear some well-meaning expert say "a tidy manure pile is a sign of a tidy mind." Even in the case of a busy riding school or other professional stable but particularly in the case of a working horse owner, a tidy manure pile is a sign of someone who hasn't got his or her priorities right. The state of your horse is far more important than the state of your muck heap.

If all your "A" jobs are done, and your horse is either contentedly munching hay in his stall, enjoying a slightly taxing exercise or socializing in the field with his friends (something you both enjoy), then it is time to get down to all those "B" jobs; now you've got nothing more important to do!

> **A tidy manure pile is the sign of warped priorities.**

You can make things even clearer for yourself by ranking jobs within categories, e.g. numbering jobs A-l, A-2, A-3 and so on, and the same with the Bs—not to put them in order of carrying them out, which you should automatically know anyway (exercising always comes before feeding, for example), but in order of importance. The idea is simply to make sure you don't waste valuable horse time or daylight hours in winter, sweeping the tack room, for instance, when the horse needs exercising. Get the horse out first, feed him, make him comfortable for the night and sweep, if you must, by electric light or by the light of your car headlights, as I've done many a time. (That teaches you to be quick, too, especially if your car battery is on its last legs!)

Juggling Jobs

In fact, working more quickly, without rushing and skimping things, is a definite asset. Imagine that it normally takes you half an hour to groom your horse and half an hour to clean his stall. Give yourself, instead, twenty-five minutes to do each task and work just that bit more quickly. You will then save ten minutes, which you can use to scrub out his feed and water containers or stay out ten minutes longer at exercise or sponge off the underside of your bridle, a job which otherwise might not have gotten done.

Hanging or traveling feeders like these are very good for providing feeds quickly to outdoor horses without having to actually go into the field and possibly fight your way through a milling herd. They can simply be slotted onto a fence rail as shown. It is advisable to feed the "boss" horse in the herd first (if you don't, he or she will just barge in anyway) and so on down the pecking-order lineup. There should be at least one more feeder available than there are horses to be fed. If there is time, it is far preferable for someone to stay and make sure the lower-ranking animals get their due. Any animal not getting his fair ration with this system should be brought out of the field and fed separately. These feeders prevent feed being tipped out into the mud, as can happen with boisterous animals fed with simple bowls or buckets, but they do not prevent feed from being scooped or tossed over the side. Note that this fencing is only two-rail post and rail. This is quite adequate for mature animals and much cheaper than the normal three- or four-rail type. The rails are inside the posts, presenting a smooth barrier, and the top rail is flush with the tops of the posts, so there is no projection to injure a horse who makes a poor job of trying to jump out.

Now imagine that you have only half an hour to spare before you have to, say, pick up your daughter from Brownies. There are two jobs which need doing: your horse needs grooming and the stable yard needs raking. Which are you going to do? You are going to groom the horse, of course! Alternatively, as that was rather a simple choice (the raking being a definite "B" job), imagine the horse needs grooming and the stall needs cleaning, both half-hour jobs, so you only have time for one of them. Why not sponge your horse's eyes, nostrils, sheath or teats and dock, dandy off the worst stable stains and mud, pick out feet into the manure basket then pick up the droppings and very worst of the bedding, scrape in some clean bedding from the sides and finally put some fresh bedding on top and banked up round the sides? That way you have insured your horse's immediate comfort and still been on time to pick up your daughter.

Without wishing to try to tell you how to run your private life, this ranking system can also be extended to your domestic chores. If it is your job to prepare the family's evening meal and to wash the car, which is the most important? The meal, of course. The car might get away with just the windows being cleaned for safety's sake.

Once you have determined job priorities, you can make out a timetable showing what you should be doing when. This might sound regimented and unnecessary, but in practice it can give wonderful peace of mind to know that you are running on schedule. Because you are doing what you should be doing when you should be doing it, you automatically know that by keeping to the timetable everything will get done in its own good time provided, of course, that no Act of God occurs to prevent it. While you are out exercising, you don't need to worry about getting the tack cleaned because you know that you have allocated a slot for it at home in the evening, perhaps while you are watching the news on T.V.

I do know people who take list making and timetabling too far and who live their entire lives by the clock. It is much better to relate it just to things other than your free time. I suppose by scheduling yourself some free time, say between 8 and 11 P.M., you are in fact scheduling that, too, but at least you needn't put "8 P.M. to 9 P.M. read book, 9 P.M. to 9.30 P.M. write thank-you

---

When down in writing, all jobs will get done.

Neglect mending a small fault, and 'twill soon be a great one.

letters for birthday presents, 9.30 P.M. to 10.30 P.M ...." and so on!

If you try the timetable system for a while, just to see how it suits you, you could well find that it really does help to keep you on course. Ultimately it will become second nature to you, and you can discard the timetable, just making out a new one if circumstances change. I still recommend a written job list, however, particularly for jobs which don't automatically need doing every day. Then you can be sure you never forget anything, which it is easy for a busy mind to do.

If you let a second-string job go undone long enough, there could come a time when it becomes an "A" job. For instance, you may leave the stable yard unraked for such a long time that it becomes a litter-strewn eyesore you suspect is harboring rodents. By then it has become an "A" and should be scheduled accordingly. It is all a matter of common sense and individual circumstance and decisions.

Buying Time, Working Smart

Saving time on particular tasks is also a matter for individual preference and circumstance. The only ways to save time on exercising are to turn out your horse for some of his exercise, to use a horse-walker if you have one available and to pony one horse while riding another. More and more professional and "full-time amateur" stables now have horse-walkers and find them a boon. Some insist that they could not run their operations without them. However, a "small" horse owner on a tight budget isn't likely to choose that option and, instead, will have to rely on one of the less expensive exercise options.

The best bedding system for horse owners in a hurry is certainly deep litter. You can pick out the droppings and replenish bedding in a dozen stalls with deep litter in the time it takes you to fully clean out one. Semi-deep litter, where droppings and the worst of the soiled bedding are removed, cleanish bedding brought in from the sides of the box and a layer of fresh material put on top, works well for many working owners, on a permanent basis or just during the week with full cleaning-out taking place only on weekends.

An item of equipment which facilitates stall cleaning is a really good, big wheelbarrow, and here the type with an oversize but light fiberglass "body" is an asset to a fairly small yard. The capacity means that you probably need just one trip to the manure pile per stall or even per every two stalls, which saves time and work. However, a single-wheeled barrow holding that much muck can be quite difficult to balance, steer and push. Manure being so heavy, it is not that difficult for the barrow to tip and spill

Good tools, well cared for, last a lifetime.

An auto-waterer has the double benefit of being a labor saver for you and a health benefit for your horse, as he will never go thirsty. Be sure the device has a drainage plug or removable "dish" for easy cleaning, and check it regularly for proper functioning.

some, if not all, of its load onto the ground, creating another unwelcome job.

We are all familiar with automatic waterers, of course, and provided they are regularly checked and have a drainage plug or removable "dish" for ease of cleaning, they are a labor saver for you and a health benefit for your horse, as he will never go thirsty. The plumbing has to be well insulated and protected, however, if the system is not to freeze in harsh weather. An added advantage of some automatic waterers is a metering system that lets you know how much your horse has drunk during the day.

Water intake is a sign of general health or disorder, so an individual meter really is a good idea.

It takes a fit, experienced groom half an hour to thoroughly groom a horse; for those not so experienced or fit (grooming is quite hard work) it takes longer. Working owners simply might not have the time to groom fully every day, and in this connection it has to be said that the horse will not die if you miss a day—or even two—provided essentials like sponging discharges from eyes, nostrils, sheath/teats and dock are attended to and, vitally important, the feet are picked out and shoes (if worn) checked twice daily.

It is true that the grooming process is, if you do it considerately, enjoyable to most horses. It stimulates the skin, gives them close contact with you and builds up a bond of trust and respect between horse and owner. I am certainly not advocating that it should be neglected as a regular thing, simply that if you are really pushed for time then a lick and a promise is quite acceptable. Grooming the horse before you exercise makes him presentable, of course. The essential point to remember is to make sure saddle area and head are free of mud and dried sweat. Otherwise tack or harness put on top of them could rub the horse sore and maybe even develop galls, not only causing pain and discomfort but making exercise difficult until the galls have healed.

If you shampoo your horse occasionally, say once a week, weather permitting, this will keep him cleaner longer and you will not need to spend so long manually grooming him on other days. Horse vacuum cleaners have been around for a long time. The most efficient are the type with a rotary brush as well as a vacuum facility. The rotary brush takes the elbow grease out of the job for you, and the vacuum prevents you from being covered in dust and dandruff. These machines also help accustom horses to being clipped as they exert a slight "pull" on the skin and make a noise from the motor, both of which clippers also do. With either machine, if your horse acts up, then stuff cotton in his ears and/or play the radio (or sing to him!) to disguise the noise. If you are tactful he will soon get used to it.

Horse vacuums can be expensive and you may well consider the expenditure ridiculous, particularly when the suggestion appears in a book devoted to saving money as well as time in horse care. However, as pointed out earlier, it is sometimes necessary to spend one in order to save the other. Spending money on an effective grooming aid will certainly save you time with daily horse-care chores, and most people who have good vacuums (the

'Tis a well-spent
penny that saves
a groat.

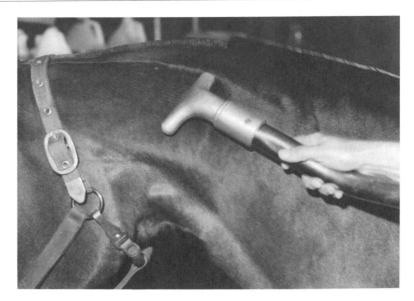

A special horse vacuum cleaner will save time with daily care. It can also save energy, something you are likely to be short of, if you are a working owner.

combined rotary brush/vacuum models) would not be without them. They also save a lot of energy, something you are also likely to be short of if you are a working owner.

Another aid to grooming which costs money but saves time is an infrared lamp in the stable aisle or in a special grooming stall. The heat lamp is useful after shampooing, which has already been recommended as a time saver. In bad weather, particularly if the horse has been out in the rain and the mud (whether ridden or just in the field), these lamps are a real boon. Simply rinse off mud, scrape off excess water, dry the heels and backs of the pasterns with an old, rough towel and leave the horse standing under the lamp while he eats his feed or hay. No blankets are needed. Even in his winter coat, he will be warm and dry in an hour, ready to be blanketed. The lamps seem to be relaxing for the horse, too, and help prevent the horse from breaking out in a secondary sweat just when you thought he was finally cooled out. There are various infrared models on the market, averaging a very few pennies an hour to run. Again, people who have them regard them as a real asset.

Laborsaving Synthetics

Synthetic fabrics and other materials are normally much easier to care for than natural ones. An exception are stable brooms—the plastic bristled ones pick up every scrap of straw in their split

Grain augured from a grain bin pours into a wheeled bucket. Labor-saving devices like this give you more free time to enjoy your horse.

ends! Natural bristles are best, and wooden handles are easier to hold, I feel. Wide-headed stable brooms are now available which have the advantage of sweeping more yard for the same amount of energy!

A field where synthetics really come into their own is that of horse clothing. New textile developments have given us the multipurpose horse blanket; they are rainproof, in many cases, or even waterproof, yet still allow condensation from a wet horse to rise up through the fabric. Sweat and moisture can evaporate easily, which was never the case with the heavy old traditional New Zealand rugs. Nowadays there are several different fabrics which perform these functions. Using a mesh anti-sweat rug under one of these rugs enables a wet horse to dry off safely on cold days.

Not all synthetic blankets have this quality, but, even so, they are much easier to launder than the traditional jute/wool night

She who cares most for "correctness" washes wool and oils leather instead of riding her horse.

rugs, heavy wool day rugs and woollen blankets of various kinds. You can take a synthetic New Zealand rug home at night, wash it in the washing machine, hang it to dry overnight and have it ready for use next day.

Nylon web tack and harness are also increasingly popular. Owners need only swish them clean in a tub of water, without having to do any laborious soaping afterwards and can save their best leather tack for important occasions. Web tack of this kind is cheaper than leather (just be sure the fittings use a strong, no-rust metal, which the best are) and very strong.

Improved plastics are also available for harness, but users report problems with excessive sweating under it in some cases. Some people also believe that it is not strong enough to be used for driving. Synthetic saddles are now firmly established in the horse world with various designs, materials, colors and sizes. You simply have to give them a good brushing and hosing down to clean them.

Adjustable-tree saddles also save money for those who ride a number of horses with markedly dissimilar back conformation or just one horse whose work causes him to change condition

A mesh anti-sweat blanket enables a wet horse to dry off safely on a cold day.

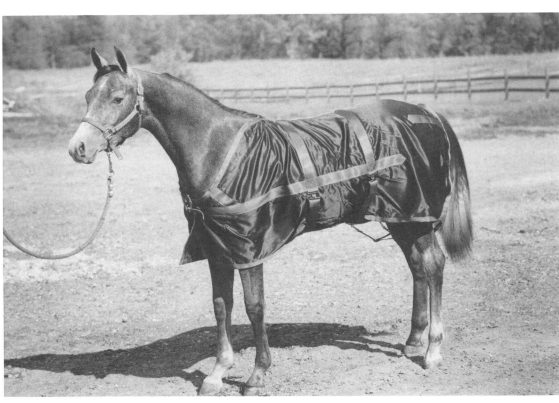

significantly during the year as he puts on weight during summer and thins down again in winter. These adjustable-tree saddles are altered by means of a key inserted at the pommel which widens or narrows the tree, enabling you to use the same saddle comfortably and safely on a range of different horse backs that may be in your stable.

Just Say No

If, after thoroughly going through your equestrian obligations with a fine-tooth comb and finding you are still not managing or that you need more time with your horse, apply time-management analysis to other areas of your life. Try listing all your responsibilities, commitments and obligations, and ask yourself whether you're taking on just a bit too much. If your family is the old-fashioned type which believes one person in the family should be responsible for most of the domestic chores, and that person is you, re-educate them to take more care of each other and to do their share of the jobs. All but the youngest children are quite capable of keeping their own rooms clean and tidy without a parent chasing after them, for instance. Spouses, too, may take a bit of re-education, but can usually be brought to see that you are entitled to your horse and your own interests and that a shared home means shared work—in other words, whoever makes the mess cleans it up!

Domestic jobs can be prioritized and allocated on an A/B basis, just like horse jobs. Take a look, too, at other aspects of your life. Do you serve on any committees? Are you an officer in an organization? Don't put yourself up for re-election next time if you want more time for your family, horse and friends. Try getting an answering machine at home so that when you really are too busy or too tired to get involved in a long gossip you can leave the machine on. More people will hang up than leave a message! On the other hand, it could mean that, since you are out so much of the time, you won't miss a really important call when it comes through.

A valuable lesson to be learned in time management is how to say "no." In all walks of life there are people only too ready to delegate tasks they don't want to do or to be responsible for to someone who will. This is standard management practice—a

> **Since thou art not sure of a minute,
> throw not away an hour.**

manager should manage and supervise, not do. So try it yourself: delegate as many unimportant and distasteful tasks as you can to someone else. If they won't accept, say gently, "Well, that's a shame. I do understand how you feel because that's how I'm fixed as well. I simply can't do the job in the future because of personal and family commitments, so I suppose it will simply have to go by the board."

Do not be finagled into carrying on a commitment you wish to shed "just until we find someone else." They rarely will. Simply give a month's notice, or whatever, and stick to it. Don't go into detailed explanations if they pry; you have already explained and the rest is none of their business. Say "no" nicely, offer to spend a limited amount of time showing someone else the ropes and then pull out the plug.

Your time is your own, after all, and no one else's.

> **Your time
> is your own
> and no one else's.**

6

Organization

Can you remember important points about your stable management or do you find yourself running things in a haphazard, hit-and-miss way? Wouldn't it be super never to be caught out, never to find that you can't go to a particular show or event because you didn't book the farrier in time and your horse's shoes are not in fit condition, and never to look silly when your vet asks certain vital questions about your horse's work or diet and you are unable to answer accurately?

Drawing Up Your Personal Plan

You can impose order on this sort of chaos by creating your own personal planning system, which I call the "master diary" system. It can be adapted for use by individual owners or by communal stables, and it runs like this:

The Diary

First buy a daily planner, at least nine by six inches, with one page allocated to each day of the year. Divide the days throughout the diary into three horizontal sections, using each portion as follows:

- The top is your "action" section for that day; use it for reminders of jobs you must do, such as "order feed," "send entries for Bumpton one-day event" or "get new spare tire for trailer."

- The middle section is for your horse's exercise and feeding programs. Line this off vertically in three columns, the first for proposed exercise, the second for feed details and the third for remarks such as "left 2nd feed; sluggish at exercise; temperature 102 degrees." This gives a record of behavior and food consumption to guide you for the future or to show your vet. During a long illness, records of temperature, pulse, respiration and general behavior, including appetite, can be vital.

- The third horizontal section is your "actual" section for recording what actually happened on that day. If everything went as planned, make a note of that. If not, put down what did occur, such as "Tansy sick, vet came p.m. . . ." plus details of treatment. In cases of illness or injury, record the quantities and names of drugs given during treatment for future reference. Also use this section to jot down routine transactions, such as "farrier came p.m., two new front shoes, hind trimmed and reset, paid $XX" or "delivery of 100 bales straw."

Data Entry

Once you've drawn all the necessary lines in your diary, transfer to it the information you wrote on your year planner, such as your vacations, major shows or events and other excursions. Your horse's fitness program can then be worked out backwards from the dates of the main competitions.

Also fill in the dates of your horse's vaccinations and boosters, teeth checks, blood tests or whatever is going to be done, fitting them around his work/holiday dates. Page back about two or

| Drive thy business or it will drive thee. |

three weeks before those diary entries, and put a note in the action section to call the vet for appointments on the appropriate dates. As you schedule those visits, note the approximate time that the vet will be arriving at the stable, so you can have the horse ready.

Ask the vet to help you plan the horse's deworming routine, and mark the appropriate dates for every deworming through-out the year, making a note two weeks before to insure that you have the drug in stock. Note the product used so that, if your vet advises it, a change to a different drug can be made to help avoid resistance developing in the parasites. If you have more than one horse, begin each entry with the individual horse's name so that you know at once to which horse it relates.

When a regular task such as shoeing has been done, be sure to mark in the diary approximately two weeks later to book the farrier again for three or four weeks after that. Then record the time of the farrier's visit on the date you've booked and a list of the horses needing his attentions.

The fourth schedule you can put in the diary, if appropriate, is your pasture-maintenance schedule, including

- land treatment,

- rotation plan,

- soil test dates and results,

- dates, types and amounts of fertilizers and lime used.

At the end of the diary, mark any events/schedules/special dates to be carried forward to next year's diary, to make sure your program continues without interruption into the new year.

> **Keep track of the details and the big days will take care of themselves.**

The Communal Record

In a communal stable, it is a good idea to get a diary with a hollow spine so you can thread some string down it, tie it to the table in the tack room and make sure it is never taken away. Owners can use it to enter when they are riding, when their horse should be cared for by someone else because the owner can't come, when the horse should be turned out, and so forth. It is also a good idea to have a pen or pencil on a string next to the diary.

If all owners get into the habit of looking at the diary, not to mention filling it in, every time they visit the stable, there will be little chance of mixups, which could result in some poor horse

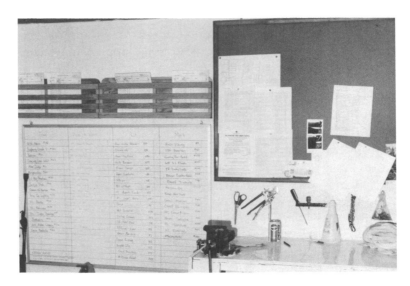

Charts and record sheets can help maintain records of horse care and management chores in any stable.

not being fed or turned out. The stable manager or owner should immediately write any messages left with her in the diary, so that whoever is responsible for seeing to things that morning, afternoon or evening will know what has cropped up in their absence.

If you use colored pens for different subjects—red for veterinary/deworming entries, blue for farrier, green for shows, for instance—you can see at a glance what is looming up in the near future, although a supply of pens like this might well "walk" in a communal yard.

An Index-Card System

When two or three horses are in your care, you might also find it worthwhile to maintain a separate alphabetical index-card system for each horse for things like shoeing, deworming and veterinary treatments, plus accidents or any unusual happenings. You will then have a record, by date, in the diary and, in more detail, by individual horse on the index cards.

These index systems are readily available from stationery and office-supply stores. They have plastic boxes with lids and alphabetical dividers (which would be needed only in very large stables) and include a supply of cards. For a small index, you can buy the cards separately and simply keep them in a plastic protector taped inside the back of the diary.

Put the horse's name in the top left-hand corner of the card, and arrange the cards alphabetically so you can go straight to the relevant one. On each card, enter the horse's

- name,
- sex,
- year of foaling,
- breeding if known,
- his date of arrival in the stable
- the owner's name, address and day and evening telephone numbers.

Down the left-hand side rule a date column, and use the space on the right for entries, like this:

June 14—Farrier, 4 new. Corn pared out, off fore. Paid $XX.

June 27—Dewormed with Brand X.

July 1—Lame. Vet came. Slight tendon strain. Two week's stall rest with 30 mins. hand walking twice daily; no grain while out of work.

> **Let he who thinks record-keeping petty be there when the auditor comes.**

A second card can be filed behind the first, giving details of the horse's fitness program and diet plus the dates of any major competitions he attended. In this way, there is a ready record of the horse's management and work history available for vet, farrier or owner, a most useful reference when illnesses or other disorders crop up in the future.

Large stables will have separate shoeing records, and "communes" should have a feed chart including instructions for all of the horses in the group-stabling arrangement, the latter normally being chalked up on a blackboard in the feed room.

With a thoughtfully planned, regularly updated diary and index-card system like these, necessary tasks, appointments and accurate records unfold before you automatically on a daily basis.

> **Record-keeping does its duties only when the keeper does his daily duties.**

(The only problem is that you are sure to have a heart attack if you lose the diary!) Provided you have remembered to write everything in as a matter of habit every day, there is only one thing you will ever have to remember, and that is to look in the diary.

Other Organizers, Additional Data

There are various organizers on the market—computer software as well as actual books—if you don't want to create your own. Some are general, and others are specialized for different equestrian disciplines, and they enable you not only to organize your daily operations but also to keep records of whatever data you need, from vaccinations to show winnings.

You should also keep careful records of

- your horse's registration numbers with different associations,

- the details of insurance policies with the policy numbers, premiums payable and renewal dates,

- the dates your dues for various clubs and societies come due.

Finally, you can simplify your phoning chores by organizing a permanent master list of useful horse-related telephone numbers, including those of your vet and at least two backups, the farrier, your most frequented tack stores, the feed supplier and the hay/straw dealer. If you're a member of a communal stable, the master list should also include all owners' day and evening

A telephone in the tack room is very convenient. Post a master list of horse-related telephone numbers, including those of your vet and at least two backups.

A well-organized tack room makes tools and gear easier to find and helps keep items clean and dry. Things well-cared-for tend to last longer, and thus you save money in the long run.

numbers which are also recorded on the individual horse's index cards, giving you a double record.

Although I said earlier that tidying the tack room was a "B" job in my book, there is a limit to the amount of disorganization which should be allowed! An untidy mess with things not in their places could cause a dangerous delay during a medical emergency, for instance. Also, it is obviously much more pleasant and satisfying when your belongings are reasonably clean and tidy. They are nicer to use, and, because well-cared-for things tend to last longer, you save money as well by reasonable care and tidiness.

The Well-Ordered Tack Room

Storage for All

In a communal yard, with or without a manager, it's not always easy to keep things just as you would want them, but owners should each be allocated a corner of the tack room for bits and pieces and their own numbered saddle and bridle places.
For such situations, I have found a free-standing six-foot kitchen cabinet invaluable. These cabinets are usually lined with easy-clean laminated board and have built-in baskets and trays which

are ideal for storing braiding equipment, veterinary supplies, grooming kits, bandages and suchlike. The lower halves usually have shelves and are quite roomy enough for storing rugs and blankets, a hand-held vacuum cleaner, clippers and buckets. Some are even deep enough and big enough for you to fix a saddle rack inside and store your saddle, if you wish, and to put a bridle hanger (an empty saddle-soap tin) on the side or inside the door. Depending on the type of handles, you may be able to put a padlock and chain through them to keep your equipment where it belongs.

Any large stable with multiple owners or just lots of horses will need storage chests or cupboards for clothing, drawers for bell boots and leg wraps and shelves for the hundred-and-one things that seem to gravitate towards the tack room in any stable.

Vet Supplies

A clean, lockable cupboard should also be available for veterinary supplies, and it is a good idea to have a list on the back of one of the doors stating what is in there. If any item is running low, it should be noted on another list and replaced before it runs out completely. A good veterinary book could be kept in the cupboard for reference, again with string threaded down the spine and tied down so the book is always where it is needed.

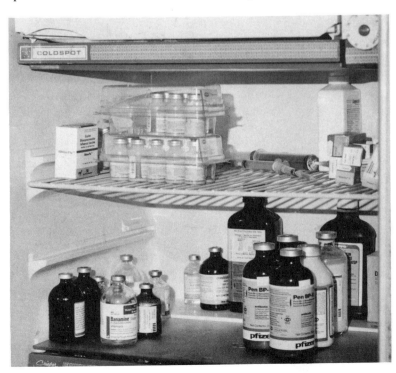

Many horse-care products require refrigeration. If you have to administer medication under your vet's supervision, a mini-refrigerator can be handy in the tack room.

Saddle-and-bridle storage
facilities should be available
in sufficient number for the
equipment on hand.

Tack Racks

Saddle-and-bridle-storage facilities should be available in sufficient number for the equipment on hand, and there are various types to choose from. Saddles should not be stored on narrow poles that fit between the seat panels, as these stretch the webbing and seat leather and spoil the saddle. Bridles should be stored on rounded holders, such as old saddle-soap tins or wooden semicircles nailed to the wall, so that the headpieces keep their shape and do not become ridged and cracked as they do when simply hung on a nail or narrow peg.

Commercial saddle racks can be obtained from tack stores and catalogs, but a simple wooden free-standing model with up-turned V-shaped saddle rest can easily be made by a handyman. If you have just one saddle and bridle, you or your handyman can

> A handyman's skill makes savings where you will.

easily fashion a wooden V-shaped rack with one end nailed to a plank which in turn is nailed firmly to the wall (presuming your wall is also wood). By affixing a bridle holder immediately underneath the shoulder-high saddle rack, you store all your tack in a compact and convenient manner.

A saddle horse is not essential for cleaning your saddle (which can be done by just resting it on your knee) but it is an asset. The most common sort usually has the upturned V structure mentioned above on a wooden stand and comes to about waist height. There may be a boot shelf underneath and drawers for tack-cleaning equipment. The saddle is rested in the normal position on top for cleaning the outside, and then the V will usually reverse so that you can rest the saddle on its back inside the V to clean the underside. To clean the bridle you can, again, simply rest it on your knee or on the table, but your job will be made simpler if you

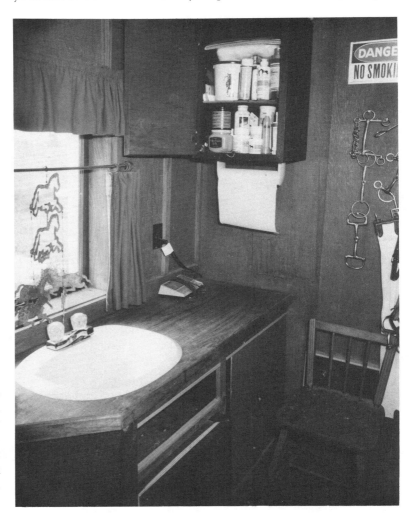

Every tack room should include a securable cabinet for veterinary supplies. Hot and cold running water should be available in the tack room for washing out wounds and cuts as well as for cleaning tack and equipment.

use a proper bridle hook hanging from the ceiling. It should be put away after use (it should unhook easily from the ceiling) so that those in a hurry do not sustain head injuries on it—painful and dangerous, as many of us know!

Utilities

Since the primary function of tack rooms is the storage of leather items, the areas should have some sort of heat to keep the temperature at a reasonable level, about 68 degrees Fahrenheit. Leather soon deteriorates in cold, damp conditions. The room can be used for drying off rugs and bandages, as well. An old-fashioned rack consisting of four or more wooden or plastic poles hauled up above head height on a pulley is very handy for this.

There should also, ideally, be hot and cold running water in the tack room. At least there should be cold tap water and some means of heating it—an electric coil or kettle, safely used. It is easier to clean grease off leather with slightly warm water (but not hot which can spoil and discolor the hide) and water warmed to body temperature is the ideal for scrubbing the scrapes and minor cuts horses have a way of turning up with. In large establishments, there may well be washing machines and dryers in the tack room for doing bandages and blankets, not to mention horse-soiled jeans and working jodhpurs, jackets and the like.

A telephone answering machine is another organizational aid for stables with multiple owners, as it will greatly facilitate message leaving and receiving. Secondhand machines are available from office-equipment shops for under $100, so it needn't be an extravagance. They are simple to operate, and all owners in a communal stable should learn how to work the machine and transfer messages left on it to the diary. If the telephone and machine are in a public place, there may be fears on the part of the barn manager/proprietor that people will be making calls at his or her expense, but a lock can easily be fitted to the dial so that the telephone is used for incoming calls only. A pay phone can be installed for outgoing calls.

> **Be miserly with your lights if you are to be happy with your bills.**

Waste-Free Feed Storage

Feed of all kinds must be stored properly, if it is to keep well. Mention has already been made of the necessity of keeping hay in a dry, airy place, as wet and direct sunshine quickly leach nutrients out of the hay and ruins it. Ideally, whether kept indoors, outdoors or half and half in an open-sided barn, it should be stored off the ground, although this may be difficult to arrange for large quantities. Wooden pallets are sometimes used for fairly small quantities; however, these permit rats to get under the fodder without being high enough to permit a cat or Jack Russell terrier to get underneath to root them out easily. A reasonable height would be one foot, if this can be arranged. New hay should be stacked, if at all possible, with space between the bales; just an inch or so makes all the difference in allowing new hay to "breathe."

The Feed Room

The feed room itself should have a dry atmosphere and should, as a matter of routine, be swept out as often as possible to avoid spilled food attracting rats and mice any more than is inevitable in farms and equestrian establishments. Hot running water, as for the tack room, is an advantage for wetting down certain feeds and for cleaning feed containers. Storage containers of whatever design should have painted on them the type of feed inside so there can be no mistakes. Horses' diets should be chalked up on a large blackboard and any changes inserted meticulously.

In large stables, a low, flat pushcart is very useful for transporting the horses' individual ration buckets from stall to stall. If each stall is numbered, then a correspondingly numbered bucket can always be used to carry the concentrate ration to the stall's occupant. However, in cases where confusion is likely to arise, such as in stables with floating populations of horses and/or attendants, the horse's name along with his daily feeding schedule and amounts can be noted clearly on an index card, which is then placed for protection inside a plastic sandwich bag or other clear plastic covering and tacked to the stall door. His box number should also be put by his name on the feed chart in the feed room. Then someone who knows which horse is which has to insure that the right horse is in the right box!

It saves walking time if "intermittent" little feed stores and tack rooms are located at, say, every sixth box stall in larger barns. In a long line of twelve stalls, for example, don't set up feed/tack rooms at the far ends of the row but put them three stalls in from each end so that each one serves the three stalls on each side of it, reducing the distance the attendants responsible for those horses have to travel.

Time can also be saved by having feed and hay hatches leading directly to the stalls' mangers and hay holders. The feed can be dispensed without the caretaker having to undo the door, dodge around the horse and reclose the stall door. It is surprising how

> **Better to feed ten cats than a single rat.**

Time can be saved by not having to enter a horse's stall every time
he needs feeding. Hatches can be provided in the walls, like this,
so that feed can be poured straight into the manger from outside or,
as in this case, from a humans-only corridor running along the backs
of the stalls. Such a facility could be added to an existing row of
stalls, space permitting, by any reasonably competent handyman or
can be incorporated into a conversion or new structure. A similar
hatch can be provided behind the hayracks so that hay can be stuffed
into them from the corridor or, easier still, from the overhead
storage loft. The feeder in this drawing is the typical plastic corner
manger (the safest, as they create no projection for the horse to
knock against) suspended in a metal frame affixed to a wooden
support or directly to the stall planks. The feeder has corner bars
to facilitate lifting it out for cleaning and also to prevent the horse
from wasting feed by rooting it into the corners and out onto the
floor.

much time this stall feature saves when you have a lot of horses to feed.

Ways to Weigh

Much feed is wasted and many horses are incorrectly fed because their feed is not weighed out properly. This can result in overfeeding or underfeeding, so it pays from both an economic and a health standpoint to have a method of weighing grain, sweet feed, pellets, etc. A large kitchen scale is quite adequate. Alternatively, a measure which holds a known weight of each type of the feed used should be kept handy. It should have neatly marked on it, preferably painted on so that it cannot easily become obscured, the amount *by weight* of each feed used, so there will no "a scoop of this and that" for feeding instructions.

Hay should also be weighed. If haynets are used, it is a simple matter to hang each net on an ordinary spring scale, available from most tack or farm-supply stores. If hay is fed in racks or loose, weigh it by placing it on an opened-out sack, bringing the four corners together and hooking them on the scale. The roughage can then be carried to the stable in the same sack to help prevent bits blowing about the grounds.

> **Overfeed by just a half-pound a day, and in one year you'll throw near four bags away.**

You'll find a measure that holds a known weight of feed to be extremely handy.

Ways with Hay

Haynets do take a bit of time to fill, but the task can be made easier by mounting two hooks (or even two large-headed nails driven partway into the wall in a slant will do), about two feet apart on a wall convenient to your stored hay at the height of the stretched-out net. Hook the mouth of the empty haynet on the hardware, pull it open to its widest extent, and stuff in the day's hay ration with your free hand.

Though an excellent space-saving idea and a major convenience once the bales are in place, the practice of storing hay and straw in a loft above the stable has two drawbacks—it can be the source of disastrous fires, and it produces much of the dust and mold spores responsible for debilitating respiratory allergies in horses stabled below. However, you may be able to overcome the fire hazard by installing a fire-resistant floor in the loft (consult your local fire department for full advice on this matter and the safety of your premises in general), and you can reduce the allergens with good stall ventilation and a generous turnout schedule for your horses.

If you do have your hay stored "on high" in some way, make sure the supplier will have an elevator to get it up there upon delivery. Otherwise you will have a very tiring and time-consuming job doing it yourself. Usually lofts have chutes or simple holes in the floors, guarded by trap doors, which drop the bales to a central aisle. However, I learned to ride when very small, at a riding school based in one of these old stables, and the trap door there opened into one of the stalls. The horse concerned did not bat an eye, but simply stepped aside as each bale came down and took a good bite out of it before it was removed. If you construct a small chute from the loft into each stall, you can deliver each horse's hay portion direct to him—either into a rack or, more wastefully, onto the floor—without having to heave and haul the heavy bales around and without creating a mess that will need cleaning up in the aisle below a central chute.

If a barn is some distance from the normal hay storage or the feed room is a long stretch from the farthest stall, you may be able to use the feed cart to transport your hay and straw. Or, if you happen to have a farm cart and a driving horse or pony in your herd, you could press him into service—he would also be useful for hauling jumps around the place. Otherwise, line the stall-cleaning wheelbarrow with unsoiled sacks and push the bales around in that. Carrying individual bales is a very tiring and inefficient way to do the job!

It's much easier to move baled hay in a wheelbarrow, than to carry it by hand.

Efficiency in Stable Layout

Most of us have little choice over our stable layout, particularly if we board our horses or keep them in rented accommodation. Where we do have a choice, however, a little thought as to how the buildings are arranged can save a lot of time and work.

The Best-Laid Plans

Any barn should be reasonably sheltered from prevailing winds. If there is no obvious prevailing wind, whatever shelter is available should be to the north and west in the United States. In other countries, shelter should be on whatever side of the yard the coldest winds come from. In general, the plains states are most subject to temperature extremes, and horses living there particularly need protection from the nearly incessant winds. Coastal areas are milder and less varying than inland regions.

Windbreaks such as trees, hedges or tough, small-weave plastic mesh will break the force of the winds rather than block them altogether as a brick wall or solid wood fence would. The latter forces the wind over the wall and into the yard, often creating a tiny whirlwind that whips up whatever lightweight objects are in its path.

> **Ten wise steps do more than 100 harried.**

It is normally recommended that the stall doors of shedrow-design stables face south so they get the sun most of the day. However, if windows or some other inlet for light is provided to the south or if there are roof skylights of some unbreakable material such as plexiglass, this will be quite adequate and will allow the stables to be situated so that the horses have a good view of what is going on or so that their position is more convenient for the human attendants.

The central-aisle floor plan for stables is ideal in countries where extremes of temperature are experienced, as horses and their caretakers can be protected from the weather nearly all the time. The barns have wide, often sliding, doors at both ends, and the stalls are lined up along both outside walls. The central aisle is usually wide enough to permit a tractor (or horse!) and cart to pass down the middle delivering feed or removing manure, which is often pitched directly from the stall into the manure spreader or cart during stall cleaning.

Guaranteeing Air Quality

The barn should be situated, if at all possible, so that it has one short end to the prevailing wind. Consequently, when the end doors are left open in summer, a cooling breeze can blow down the length of the barn, but in winter, when the doors are closed, a comparatively small area is presented to the winds, so reducing their chilling effect.

Here again, every opportunity should be taken to provide ventilation outlets, such as

- ridge-roof ventilators,

- extra opening windows or shutters high up on the walls,

- top-half doors in the outside walls at the back of each stall so the horses can be allowed to look out in summer—a definite advantage from the horses' points of view.

> **The same wind that in summer is a boon, in winter is a beast.**

In fact, full Dutch doors can be provided to allow individual entrance to each box from outside. Apart from avoiding possible congestion in the center aisle, this will provide another exit for each horse in case of fire or other emergency.

A simple test of ventilation is to spend some time in the open air and then walk into an occupied stable. If you notice a significant difference in the interior air, if it feels noticeably warm, stuffy or—worse—smelly, you can be sure that ventilation is inadequate and that the horses kept in the stalls are suffering for it.

Desirable Dimensions

Other buildings can be converted for use as stables, of course, and it is hoped that some of the accompanying illustrations will inspire ideas for unconventional but healthy and convenient horse accommodations and building conversions. Whatever method is used, an important point to remember is that the horses should have as much headroom as can be allowed. Many prefabricated box stalls allow only seven feet, six inches to the eaves, which I feel is not high enough for either safety or ventilation. A twelve-foot eaves height should be aimed at wherever possible, to allow for a rearing horse. Lower heights are obviously acceptable for small horses and ponies.

In a line of conventional loose boxes, typical of racetrack shedrows, it helps to have some kind of overhang roughly two yards wide to protect the horses from rain or snow and from hot summer sun. It is usual to have windows in these boxes on the same side as the door to prevent cross-drafts. However, in hot weather a cross-draft is an advantage, so windows should be provided on the back wall or at least shutters or some other method—even just a removable plank of wood—of providing a welcome breeze in the stall in summer.

Adequate floor space is also needed, and long narrow boxes should be avoided as they do not allow the horse to lie flat out in safety to sleep. Horses have an inborn need for space and a love of movement. They are not happy in confined stables, and for this reason, although standing or tie stalls are still in use in some establishments (and may be acceptable in those where the animals habitually get a great deal of exercise each day), I cannot recommend them for privately owned horses, most of whom receive comparatively little exercise. Even when such a horse is turned out for several hours, I still feel that stalls are unacceptably restricting for most animals and can be very stressful to their occupants. Generally speaking, a floor space of about twelve feet by fourteen feet should be adequate for a horse of about sixteen hands high (more if he is of an active nature) and about twelve feet by ten feet for ponies.

Shed Strategies

Where horses are "yarded" (as described in Chapter 1), hay hatches in the back walls of the sheds make the filling up of communal hayracks much easier. There is no need to remove sliprails or open gates, fight your way through a small herd (even two!) of horses grabbing at the hay before you have had a chance to put it in the racks and then retrace your steps again. Yarded

> **Build ceilings so low to bump at first jump, or so tall rearing horses can't touch them at all.**

horses, however, may need concentrates fed separately to insure that each one gets his correct ration and, although this may be difficult to arrange, yarding saves so much time and work in other respects that it is not a serious disadvantage. Yards with run-in sheds for shelter can conveniently be made to continue on into the paddock or pasture, so avoiding the need for an additional field shelter. Depending on the exact position of the shed, it may be useful to people to have access into it for themselves and for the horses from the stable yard, and also to have some means (probably strongly constructed gates or sliprails) of keeping the horses in the shelter itself without access to the yard/paddock, perhaps in cases where either is waterlogged due to excessive rainfall. Left to themselves, most horses will spend most of their time outside in yard or paddock rather than where we think they should want to be—in the shelter. However, if the shelter is large enough the horses will still be happier in there together than stabled individually.

For paddocks with simple field shelters in them, one shelter can, with a little imagination and depending on the exact layout of your premises, be made to serve three paddocks or more. The same goes for watering points. When housing your horses in sheds, you still have to pick up the manure, dispense the hay and inspect the horses twice daily, so it is more convenient and timesaving to have the shelters as near as reasonably possible to the main barn to cut down on hauling distances for hay/bedding and other gear and supplies.

> **Begrudge not the private feeding of the shed-kept horse; thou couldst be pitching manure instead.**

Securing Yourself Against Loss

Security of your premises can obviously do a lot to prevent your ever suffering the psychological trauma and financial losses that thievery and vandalism inflict on their victims. It is true that if thieves or vandals really want to get into a place they will get in, no matter how good the security and whatever the premises, so the best we can do is make things difficult for them by effective security measures. Most thieves and vandals are opportunists— they will select the place which offers easy pickings rather than the one which will cause them problems.

Police Call

The police are an excellent source of general security advice and may know of regional or local security schemes for preventing horse-related crimes, so contact the crime prevention department of your local force for advice on beefing up your security. They will come and inspect your premises at no charge and tell you where security is weak and what you can do to improve it, recommending products and measures to help you foil unwanted visitors to your premises. I have always found their advice practical and full of common sense. They won't say that your only hope is to install thousands of dollars worth of burglar alarms, for instance, but will suggest economical alternatives—maybe a cheaper burglar alarm. They will tell you what types of fencing, doors, locks, windows and so on to use and will even suggest surfacing for paths (gravel, for instance, makes a noise when trodden on and would quickly alert a guard dog).

> **He who steals your property robs you of your peace of mind.**

Tack-Room Tactics

Ideally, tack rooms should be accessible only from the house, although this might be impractical or, indeed, impossible where the house is not near the stable. For the maximum security, tack-room windows should have metal bars on them, not weak tubular rods or wood and should have two different five-element mortise locks. The door should open outward, not inward, to make it difficult for it to be "shouldered" in, and door and window frames should be very strongly fitted into the walls. If there is only one brick or stone building on the place, it is probably best to use it for tack and harness. This building should not back on to a public highway.

Some owners in communal boarding stables feel it's better to take at least their saddles and bridles home with them for safety's sake. Not all stables, particularly the smaller, "informal" barns, have adequate security precautions for tack, and there is a booming trade in stolen tack and harness.

Marked Tack

Marking your tack and equipment with a permanent identification number as a deterrent to crime and a means of making good your claim of ownership in the event of thievery is a sound idea, at least in principle. However, in the absence of a national registry of such numeric identities, it's difficult to decide on the numbers that will be most likely to get a recovered stolen item back in your hands. Although your social security number is unique and stays with you for life, the Social Security Administration will not disclose the name and address of the person assigned a particular number. So if your stolen saddle resurfaces for sale, and some sharp-eyed shopper notices your social security number engraved on the stirrup bar and decides to investigate to see if the rightful owner has been the victim of tack theft, he has no way of tracing the number to you. Driver's license numbers are traceable, but that identification is useless if you move to another state and let your previous license lapse. Using your street number and zip code clearly identifies a stolen item's origin, without requiring the assistance of such agencies as the Motor Vehicles Administration, yet it's invalid the moment you move.

In fact, what do you do with identifying marks during the legitimate exchange of other equipment (as gifts or for second-hand sale)? Any mark that's easily expunged or changed is useless from the standpoint of security, so the permanent mark may just have to be a nuisance to the item's next-in-line owner.

Horse Identification

To identify an even more precious commodity—your horse or horses—you may want to try freeze marking, the implantation of a microchip that can be "read" with a special scanner, a hoof "brand" burned in by the farrier every six months or so or, as is the custom in the West, burning on a ranch brand with a hot iron.

Freeze marking, with the identifying number usually put along the crest of the neck where the mane can be used to hide it, is routinely used to brand "wild" horses rounded up and offered for public sale by the Bureau of Land Management and is also the preferred identification of some registries, such as the International Arabian Horse Association. The unalterable, highly visible mark can be extremely successful in not only restoring stolen or escaped animals to their rightful owners but in preventing theft in the first place. Slaughterhouses and auction yards usually require proof of ownership before accepting a freeze-marked horse for sale or slaughter.

If any form of permanent identification is to protect horses from being stolen and sold, there must be awareness of the identifying technique among the general horse public, law-enforcement officers at the local, state and federal levels, the usual outlets for stolen animals (auctions and slaughterhouses) and, of course, the thieves themselves. A national registry of identification numbers, brands or microchip data is also essential for recovery of stolen animals transported across state lines.

**Which would you rather:
a few dollars for identifying
or thievery that leaves you crying?**

Freeze-marking with a number along the crest of the neck is unalterable and highly visible. The technique can be instrumental in recovering animals and in preventing theft.

The horse-identification industry in the United States has been advancing in fits and starts since the early 1970s, with related companies going into and out of business with some regularity. If you decide to invest in one of the more recent identification procedures to protect your horses, look for information and advertisements in the equestrian press and then check out each company's track record for serving clients in what is always an emergency situation and for assisting in the recovery of missing and stolen animals.

Rapid Response

Stolen horses can be slaughtered within hours—by the time you discover the theft, your horse may be dead—and slaughterhouses cannot possibly check on the legal ownership of every horse brought to them. And once a horse has passed through a public auction and been bought by a patron, the only way the original, rightful owner can reclaim it is to buy it back from the purchaser. This is the law, unjust though it seems. For these reasons, you need to act immediately upon realizing that your horse is missing. Organizing yourself in advance for this type of emergency will give you the jump start that might mean your horse's survival:

• Compile a list of the names, addresses and telephone numbers of all slaughterhouses, auctions and horse dealers in your region.

• Take good-quality snapshots of all your horses, showing them from both sides, front and back, with close-ups of any distinguishing marks or scars, and of each of their four chestnuts (those callus-like growths on the insides of his upper forelegs and lower hind legs), which are as individual to horses as our fingerprints are to us.

• Keep enough copies of your photographs, clearly showing any identifying marks, to distribute throughout the horse community and to slaughter operators and horse dealers.

• Keep a list of the appropriate contact numbers at your local police department, animal-control department and horse-rescue group (if there's one in your area) so you can immediately phone to report a missing horse.

Crime-Stopping Steps

There has been a tragic increase in the number of seemingly senseless attacks on horses within the past decade. Brands, freeze marks and other sorts of identification will not stop such attacks, as the horses concerned are not stolen or even removed from their premises. Security of those premises is, therefore, a common-sense focus for your efforts. Horses most at risk are those in isolated fields, possibly near roads, which give vandals easy access, but away from buildings, particularly inhabited houses, and those stabled in barns where there is no supervision for extended periods and/or there are no living quarters for humans on the premises and which are, therefore, deserted for most of the time, especially at night.

If you're concerned about tightening up the security of your stable to ward off vandalism or thievery, consider taking the following steps:

• A big guard dog—preferably two—with a bark to match roaming loose at night (but obviously with access to adequate, dry shelter) can be a strong deterrent, but check the position with your crime-prevention officer because if the dogs bite anyone, even someone who has actually broken on to your premises, you can be held liable for their injuries. Geese make excellent guards as they can be noisy and vicious without inflicting the same kinds of injuries as dogs, and they are less prone to bribery with food!

• Thieves and vandals can easily cope with wooden and wire fencing; thick, prickly hedges and stone walls are much more difficult for them but uncommon in American farms. Have paddock gates opening on to your premises rather than on to public right-of-ways. Make all gates the type which cannot be lifted off their hinges, and padlock and chain them securely at both ends.

• By leaving halters on your horses, whether they're stabled or turned out, you're simplifying things for thieves and vandals. Remove halters from horses whenever no attendants will be nearby (although you want the halters easily accessible, especially for stabled horses, in case they have to be moved quickly). This is one instance where a hard-to-catch horse or pony is a definite advantage. A pastured herd could well have its own protector in the form of a horse known to attack people!

• Have some kind of alarm bell or lighting system wired to the gate and/or fence to surprise intruders when they set it off. This can be quite simply arranged with a car battery, a simple make-and-break contact and a strong light.

• Connect the stable-yard light to a switch in the house so that it can be turned on easily at any suspicious sound or movement. Sensor-operated security lights that are activated by motion are now commonplace for houses and other premises and are very reasonable in price considering the security they offer.

• Get to know neighbors near your stable and ask them if they would let you know if strangers seem to be loitering or frequently visiting the area. Give them your telephone numbers, and send them at least a card at Christmas for their troubles!

• When you travel to shows and other events, don't leave your vehicle unattended and don't scatter equipment around where anyone can pick up an item and walk off with it. Never leave the keys in the ignition, and certainly do not leave animals unattended in the horse van or trailer. Even in the stable area, always have at least one person watching the animals and equipment.

Thieves hate being surprised, having their presence heralded and making them subject to identification It's true that many horses are taken in broad daylight, particularly from outlying fields and yards where no one actually lives, but you cannot cover every eventuality. All you can do is make it difficult for thieves to carry out their nefarious plans under cover of dark.

> When geese are your guards, there's no bribing with treats.

7

Care of the Horse

The purpose of this book has been to discuss how to look after horses while spending as little time and money as possible. When I spoke on this subject at a seminar before the book was finished, it was pointed out to me that it's all very well to cut corners if you know exactly where to cut them without harming the horse. To do this, you need to be a knowledgeable horseperson. Advising novices to cut down on certain tasks could, it was suggested, lead to important areas of management being skimped due to lack of understanding. It is like learning to recognize injury or illness in a horse: How can we know what is abnormal if we do not know what is normal? It is because of this suggestion that this final chapter on basic care and management has been included.

There are many books on how to look after horses and ponies. and they are all slightly different due to their authors' having differing opinions on various aspects of the subject. One of the best books on general horse care and management now available is *The Complete Book of Horse Care* by Tim Hawcroft, BVS, MACVS (Breakthrough Publications). It is more advanced than most management books and covers, in an easily understandable way, topics often discussed only in veterinary books for horse owners.

The following discussion of the most important aspects of basic care and management of the horse inevitably conveys my own knowledge and opinions on the subject gained over many years of practice, observation and study. I hope it will be useful to readers in helping them to decide where to cut the corners mentioned earlier, so enabling them to care properly for their animals while saving both time and money.

The days are long gone when stables could provide one groom per two or three horses. The economics of horse keeping in the latter part of the twentieth century preclude the continuance of many of the practices devised by the employers and managers of the nineteenth century (many of whose methods live on in present-day textbooks and establishments where "traditional" ways persist). There simply isn't the time and money to perform some of them and, fortunately for the working horse owner or any owner who hasn't all day to devote to his or her horse or horses, there are many "traditional" tasks which can safely be skimped or skipped without any harm to the horse.

Some of the ideas and methods I recommend may seem like sacrilege to purists and traditionalists, but they have withstood years of practice with no detriment to the many different types of horses and ponies involved.

> At a great bargain,
> pause a while;
> many have been
> ruined by buying
> great pennysworth.

> Ill customs and
> bad advice are
> seldom forgotten.

Horse Psychology and Physiology

The horse is a herd animal and an animal of the wide open spaces. Most members of the horse family (and this includes asses and zebras, as well) do not do well either mentally or physically when living alone. There are odd exceptions, but most equidae thrive on company. Similarly, most of them do not do well when kept confined. Horses are not cave dwellers like apes (human apes, anyway) and do not live in dens like dogs. They are, by natural evolution, nomadic within a certain territory. They have a natural love of and need for space, company, movement and an all-round view. Life in a stable is highly unnatural to them, and too much of it certainly causes mental and physical problems.

Many of the stable vices we normally attribute to boredom can in truth be blamed accurately on the frustration and distress of

This drawing shows ideal facilities for stables large and small. The play area in the foreground was reclaimed from a boggy piece of ground by excavating and selling off the topsoil, laying bricks, gravel and finally fine shale to create relatively dry, secure footing for the horses. The animals have a shed, bedded in deep litter, and haynets rather than a built-in rack. The door in back of the shed allows easy access for people, but the horses are brought in through the gate on the left. Water is provided by hose to the plastic garbage can tied to the fence and rammed into an old tractor tire for security. If the gate to the adjoining field (on the right) is left open, the horses can come and go as they wish; there is no need to provide another shelter in the field as they can always get to the one in the play area. When ground conditions are bad, the gate is closed, and the horses restricted to the play area/shed complex, which they prefer to being kept stabled. Note how the fence between field and play area has an extra rail at a horse's shoulder height running along on the field side for safety. This small establishment shows how imaginative thinking and consideration for the horses can provide ideal facilities that benefit both the animals and their caretakers.

overconfinement. Although a horse already confirmed in a particular vice may be difficult or impossible to cure completely, most horses I have come across improve tremendously when managed in a more natural manner. Not only do vices of various kinds lessen or disappear, but the horses' temperaments improve where they have previously been suspect or downright nasty. The sad yearning so apparent in many stable-kept horses and the dull resignation shown by just as many others are replaced by a very obvious air of happiness and calm contentment. The horses are also much more interested in life in general, more amenable to their human handlers and more willing in their work.

I am not advocating that all horses should be "freed of their shackles," as it were, and kept permanently at pasture with all the disadvantages this entails for both horse and owner. What I do know, however, is that horses become much easier and more pleasant to look after when they are happy and, from a working owner's point of view, burdens of caretaking are considerably lessened by keeping horses in a manner suited to their mental as well as their physical needs.

We all know that one of the most often quoted rules of feeding is "feed little and often" to follow the horse's natural way of taking in and digesting food. We make an effort to meet his needs in this respect, but many of us appear to overlook completely his needs with respect to mental health and happiness which are so easily met by turning him out into a grass paddock for some time each day, allowing him a reasonable amount of freedom. If grass is unavailable, freedom and the chance to do as he likes for a period can be provided by turning him into a prepared riding area such as an indoor arena, outdoor ring or just one of the play areas already mentioned.

To make it a proper job, he should have the company of a compatible horse or pony. This turning-out period should be regarded as of equal importance to other daily requirements, such as feeding, stall cleaning and, certainly, ridden or driven exercise. Horses may certainly enjoy the work we ask them to do and many, in fact, feel left out and neglected when not in work, but exercise under constraint is not a substitute for liberty.

The provision of liberty needs adequate facilities, but as suggested, it should not be beyond the means of most stables to provide them, using a little imagination. Of course, even hardy crossbreds and ponies are not happy when turned out for long periods in an exposed field that offers no real shelter from driving rain, wind, sun and flies, especially if they are alone. In truly natural conditions, animals do have the chance to seek out the shelter of trees, shrubs and the terrain, all of which help break the force of the wind and weather and offer some shade in summer.

Natural social contact is also much more important than many owners seem (or wish) to acknowledge. Horses feel more secure in the company of their own kind. In the wild, when herds were

> The horse thinks one thing, and he that saddles him another.

subject to predators (as they still are in some parts of the world), there was safety in numbers. If there are a lot of you running together, the predator, with luck, will pick someone else out of the crowd for his dinner. This need for company is very strong in horses, domesticated or feral, although some do seem to survive contentedly alone. However, my experience of those formerly kept alone is that they almost invariably prefer company when given a choice.

Even stallions usually turned out alone are better when they can see other animals around them. Those who habitually run with their mares have a much more balanced, calm and natural outlook toward life than those used solely in hand and never allowed to associate naturally with their own kind. Stallions who are turned out with an elderly, experienced, nonbreeding female companion, even when they must serve their "real" mares in hand, again have a much happier and more sensible outlook on life than those deprived of what is, in effect, their birthright.

A Taste of Freedom

It is obvious, therefore, that the opportunity to move around at liberty, even in a small paddock or a dirt play area, for a few hours a day is far better than being confined to a stable most of the time. Two friends can be turned together into even quite a small area and will exercise each other and be company, too. Most stables have the odd unused area, or could sacrifice some space somewhere—preferably adjoining a box stall or with some kind of shed in it—which could be converted into such an exercise area.

The top soil (if the area is earth) could be sold or used elsewhere on the premises and the area paved with bricks and subsequently covered with some suitable material, such as fine gravel, and topped with used bedding (minus droppings), stone dust or something similar. Such a facility can be a boon to any establishment but particularly to a working owner short of time for exercising or, indeed, to anyone who believes, as I do, that horses are better off with as much liberty as is reasonably possible.

Paved pens of this kind are invariably useable when paddocks and pastures are simply too muddy for turnout, or they can be used to save the grass or to give horses some sense of freedom without their getting filthy and creating the extra job of cleaning them up. Just a few hours a day in such a "yard" in addition to normal exercise can make our job that much easier by keeping the horses saner and happier than most are when confined continually to their stalls except for under-saddle exercise. As the

> **Even a little liberty is better than a lot of stall.**

horses will choose to spend most of their time in the outdoor area, their stall bedding is saved, making less work for us at stall-cleaning time and less expenditure on bedding material.

Even just moving about slowly is better for the horse's physical health than being kept stabled and standing still for the very long periods to which many horses are subjected. Because of the boost to the circulation, horses who normally stock up, for example, do not seem to experience the edema in their lower legs when given small play areas like this. And, of course, the fresh air is of undoubted benefit, even to horses not prone to respiratory allergies to stable dust and mold spores.

It is, therefore, an advantage to the horse and to his busy working owner if a little thought can be brought to bear on the subject of facilities that offer both liberty and company.

Tethering

A little imagination will produce all sorts of exercise facilities to help the working owner at any time of year and provide his or her horse with enough exercise to keep him happy, healthy and contented. A number of such facilities have already been discussed in this book, with the exception of one other—tethering.

Tethering a horse and leaving him is, in my opinion, a very poor way to manage him. I recommend it only as being a suitable way of using some spare patch of unfenced grass about the place and letting the horse have just a bit more movement than he would get in his stall. Even so, the horse should be tethered only if he's of a steady and sensible nature and it is certain he won't be subject to vandalism, even from the stable dog or loose ponies. He should not be left out unsheltered in adverse weather conditions such as hot sun, fly weather, rain/sleet or wind. If you decide to try tethering, use a neck strap rather than a halter. Many horses seem to prefer them and don't pull on them as much as with halters, plus they're cheaper. The tether stake—a swivel type that's at least a yard long—should be driven very firmly into the ground.

Fencing Options

Fencing is, of course, important for any sort of enclosure, and its high cost is one reason turnout facilities are so limited or even lacking on many establishments where horses are kept.

Love your neighbor; yet don't pull down your hedge.

Traditional fencing for horses is made of timber posts and boards.

Board Fencing

Traditionally, the most popular and suitable fence for horses has been timber posts and boards. Board fencing can be quite expensive to install, but economies can be made where it is to be used for mature horses. Here, two-rail fencing is quite adequate, with the top rail at the horses' back height and the next about halfway between it and the ground. For broodmare paddocks and pastures, three- and probably four-rail fencing will be needed to stop foals from getting through the fence or rolling under it and ending up, panic-stricken, away from mom on the other side. In such cases, the bottom rail should be no more than one foot from the ground.

Among the most expensive form of fencing in terms of both money and time for maintenance, the white-painted board fence has to be repainted regularly—at the first sign of peeling—if you want it to look topnotch. And in fact, from an ecological point of view, white fencing is an eyesore, a blot on the landscape that I feel we can well do without in every way.

Nevertheless, preserving the wooden parts of your fence is very important. Creosote can be hazardous to horses and to people who come in contact with it during or after application. In fact, the stinky, black deterrent to rot and insects is now a federally regulated chemical that not every Tom, Dick and Harriet can go buy and apply. More modern preservatives may not be much safer, but the pretreated lumber available through most building-supply outlets and fencing contractors does withstand the elements and wood-loving insects far longer and with less maintenance than untreated wood.

A point against any board fence, whether it is hardwood or softwood, treated or plain, is that some horses still chew it. Horses often do this if their diets are short of bulk—when the grass is poor, for instance—or when they are bored—no graze, no hay, no company, simply nothing else to do. Young horses might chew a fence when teething and, although this is a temporary phase, it can last quite long enough for them to weaken and ruin the appearance of the wooden rails. It might be considerate to provide young horses with a "teething post," such as I once saw on a top Thoroughbred breeding farm, in one corner of the field where they cannot bump into it.

Post-and-Rail Fencing

A scenic sort of fencing that is safe for horses, post and rail requires no painting and needs no nails (a hazard to hooves when left behind on the ground by workmen) during construction or repair. Most commercial varieties are made of treated wood, thereby reducing rot and insect damage and extending the fence's life. But like all wood on horse farms, it may still be damaged by chewing. Unless post-and-rail fencing uses hefty components and deeply planted posts, the nail-free construction can begin to fall apart rather early in its life as the uprights shift and the rails sag.

Woven-Wire Fencing

Square or rectangular woven-wire fencing is widely used, from the ordinary "large-weave" agricultural variety to a type specially made for horses with smaller meshes near the bottom, ostensibly too small to allow a hoof pass through. In my experience the latter type is not much more effective in this regard than the wire with larger openings, and I cannot recommend either type because of their likelihood of catching horses' heels and pasterns.

Small-mesh (far too small for even a foal foot to get caught) diamond fencing is excellent—but not the weak, wobbly, plastic-

> **Well-made fences are investments, not expense.**

Woven-wire fencing is widely used, and white boards can be used with it to enhance visibility.

covered sort used in so-called "security" fencing which almost anyone can break through by either cutting or unraveling it. Used extensively on Thoroughbred breeding farms, this wire fencing is tough, durable, highly visible and relatively short on maintenance demands. Naturally, it's the most expensive type of wire fencing you can install.

Electric Fencing

Portable, inexpensive, quick and easy to install, electric fencing can be used successfully for horses, but it does have some major drawbacks:

• Its low visibility makes it a hazard for animals and people not aware of its presence; frightened horses stampeding through it may escape unharmed if the wire breaks (not terribly likely) but if it doesn't give way, it can inflict grievous wounds.

• The metal rods often used to support the electrified wire have been known to impale horses who jump on or were forced into them.

• Your animals' escape may be the first notice you get that the charger has failed or that the current has been grounded out and the fence is no longer electrified.

A newer type of electric fencing resembling a shiny metal or brightly colored ribbon, sometimes with neon-colored plastic strips or "flashes" on it, takes care of the visibility problem, and safety "caps" for the potentially piercing posts can also take some of the worry out of this form of fencing.

Electric fences are especially useful

• inside existing fencing that is either dangerous or inadequate,

• for dividing up a large permanently fenced pasture into smaller strips for rotational grazing,

• as a don't-touch-me reminder on the top rail of wood fences for horses who chew on, lean against, run along or otherwise damage permanent materials.

Electric fencing can be used successfully for horses, but its low visibility and the metal rods post serious hazards.

Horses should be correctly introduced to electric fencing. To do so, damp their noses, lead them up to it and press their noses against the charged wire. They should receive enough of a shock to send them sharply backwards without actually being hurt. Lead them all along the fence, repeating the operation at intervals, and you should soon find that when you try to get them to "sniff" the wire, they refuse pointblank.

High-Tensile Wire Fencing

An increasingly common fencing—probably because of its relative economy—for horses is multiple strands of plain heavy-gauge wire stretched on permanently installed wooden posts. Provided it is kept tightly stretched (hence the "tensile" in its name), it is a fair fencing. It's not terribly visible, but attaching "flutter" strips of colored plastic solves that problem. Maintenance time and expenses are low, and if you electrify the top strand, horses shouldn't do any damage by leaning or rubbing.

Now for the downside: If one strand of the high-tensile wire gives way for any reason, it will sag along the whole of its length, lowering the fence if it is the top strand. Whichever strand it is, it will leave swathes of loose wire about for the horses to get tangled up in—and they probably will. With a shod horse, there is also some chance that while pawing the wire or playing near the fence, he could get a wire wedged between the heel of the shoe and his hoof. More than likely he'll be panic-stricken, injuring himself in his struggles to get free, either ripping off the shoe or severely straining tendons, ligaments or muscles. And the fence can't help but be damaged in the struggle, as well.

Of course, the trapped hoof or caught leg is a real possibility with almost every type of wire fencing used—and there's many a scarred heel and pastern out there to prove it. If there's a wire fence on the property where your horse is pastured, keep a pair wire cutters handy and always stored in the same place so that everyone in the stable knows where to find them in an emergency.

> **Wire cutters may ruin a fence but save a horse.**

Synthetic Fencing

Thirty-year guarantees; install and forget; flexible, non-splintering rails. The recent innovations in synthetic fences offer solutions to all the fencing headaches horse keepers have been struggling with since stone walls and hedges went out of fashion. Plastic (PVC) fences may be able to pass for white board fences but, guaranteed by their manufacturers for at least a few decades, they do the job without the rot, constant repairs and frequent

Though expensive, plastic (PVC) is a popular, low-maintenance fence material. This home-made fence, using sections of PVC plumbing pipe, is attractive and durable.

repainting. Rubber strips, easily nailed to wooden posts, don't deteriorate in the weather and give, rather than splinter, if a pasture occupant blunders against them. Fencing made of parallel strands of heavy-gauge wire joined by weather-resistant plastic has many of the same advantages as rubber strips, but it comes in more fashionable colors and looks more plank-like (from a distance). This flexible-rail fencing is attached to its posts

Without question, barbed wire is unsuitable for horses, an invitation to serious wire cuts. In addition, it's a weak form of fencing.

similarly to high-tensile wire and requires occasional tightening with a rachet device to keep it taut.

As you'd expect, most types of synthetic fencing are quite expensive to buy and possibly to install. If they live up to their billings in terms of durability and low-to-no maintenance, they may be money-savers in the long run since they can all be picked up and moved along with your horses if you ever change residences.

General Fencing Tips

As with many other aspects of horse care, or perhaps with fencing especially, trying to save money at the expense of your horse's health and safety is no bargain at all. Flimsy, poorly installed fences and those made of hurtful materials are accidents waiting to happen, either through direct injury to your horse or through his escape into a dangerous, unfenced world. The fencing guidelines below are good for whatever type of fence you maintain or install:

> **The most important part of the fence post is the part you don't see.**

• Beware of barbed wire, which is quite unsuitable for horses. A single strand along the top of a board or woven-wire fence poses the least danger and may deter leaning or chewing, but a fence with multiple strands, especially a poorly maintained fence with loose, looping wire, is an invitation to serious wire cuts of your horse's lower legs.

• Fence posts should be sunk into the ground for at least 40 percent of their length (for the typical eight-foot post, you'd bury approximately 3.5 feet of it). It doesn't take many fanny scratchings by a half-ton or more of horse to loosen and tilt an inadequately sunken post and disrupt the attached fencing. Wobbly posts also make fence repairs and general maintenance difficult or impossible, so don't economize on the length of posts.

• Attach the rails (wooden or synthetic) or wires of any type fence on the inside (pasture or paddock side) of the posts. This arrangement presents as smooth a barrier as possible to galloping horses, so they do not sustain injuries from banging against the posts (usually with their shoulders and possibly with their hips), and prevents the rails or wires from being pushed off the posts by leaning or rubbing horses.

• If a single fence is used to separate two fields, run a single rail/wire at point-of-shoulder height on the side where the posts are "exposed" for the reasons given above.

• Set a rail or rails across the corners of a field to "round them off" and steer galloping horses out of the potential trap. Avoid creating sharp (acute) corners in your fence lines as one horse can easily hem in another during a kicking match, and the one with no escape could be seriously injured.

• Walk (or ride) your fences regularly, possibly once a week if a large portion is not easily visible from the stable, to take care of any minor repairs before they become major trouble.

Whatever your expenditure on fencing may be, it should be regarded as an essential investment, to enable your horse to be turned out, increasing his good health and pleasure in life and easing the time/work burden on you.

Watering

A horse can survive very much longer without food than he can go without water. Fresh water is, after air, the world's most vital resource, and lack of it leads to dehydration and many other problems. Dehydration can occur in winter when horses' water sources are iced over, as well as in summer when excessive sweating and inadequate fluid intake can quickly lead to an internal shortage.

The Essential Nutrient

A horse's body consists of approximately 70 percent water (the younger the horse, the more water his body contains). The cells of the body are bathed in and filled with water-based fluids. Blood is, of course, mainly water, as are lymph and the digestive juices; the eyes contain water and the horse's joints are lubricated by a fluid called synovia. Even hoof and hair contain water.

Mares obviously use water to make milk, and the horse's excretory systems depend on fluids: Urine transports waste products out of the body, droppings are moist and sweat contains waste products. Sweat is also important as a regulator of body temperature. Heat is lost by the evaporation of warm sweat into the surrounding, air. Water is even lost from the body in the vapor expelled from the lungs with each breath. Given this continual water use and loss, horses require adequate supply of this essential nutrient in every twenty-four hour period.

> **When the well's dry we know the worth of water.**

All the normal feeds we give our horses contain some water, and of course grass contains more water than anything else. However, an additional, purely fluid supply is needed: Ponies and horses can drink anywhere from six to fifteen gallons a day depending on size, work and weather.

If a horse is short of water, his homeostatic mechanism will dole out the precious interior fluids to the most vital bodily processes after robbing them from the second-string concerns. The skin will give up fluids for the sake of digestive tract, for instance. That's why you can test for dehydration in your horse by pinching the skin on the point of his shoulder; if the pinch flattens back out immediately, his fluid levels are fine. If it remains peaked, his vital juices are running low. Horses working hard in high temperatures and/or very low humidity are particularly prone to dehydration, especially the endurance and event types whose work is prolonged.

Scheduling a Drink

In the wild, equidae normally drink early in the morning and in the evening, when possible, often trekking long distances to water holes. Zebras in southern Africa have been said to go regularly for three days or so without drinking, apparently without suffering significantly. Even today, there are establishments that water their horses only at morning and night and after work (before feeding). This is a job in itself, either carrying water to the horses or taking them to drink from a communal trough (not the most hygienic of practices).

However, this is not the sort of lifestyle we would want our domesticated horses and ponies to experience, and most books on management recommend that water always be available to the horse in stable and field. Much time and work is saved by having automatic waterers in the stables, and the horses can drink a little whenever they wish. People who say horses should have their water removed before feeding do have a point, but it is my experience that horses with water always before them do not take a long drink even straight after work.

Some horses do like to drink immediately after and sometimes even during feeding, but again I have not found this to be harmful when water is always available. Feed-time intake is normally just small amounts that in no way seem to hinder digestion and may actually stimulate the digestive juices.

Automatic Waterers

A drawback with ordinary automatic waterers is that you cannot tell how much or how little a horse is drinking. As water intake is a valuable sign of health and disease, it is worthwhile seeking out the type of waterer which has a small meter attached so you can see at a glance how much is being used. Also, a good type of appliance is one with a plug hole at the bottom so that it can easily be drained and cleaned. The type of plug with a little inset handle is impossible for the horse to pull out.

Horses are not generally happy with the nose-operated cattle type of waterer where they have to press down a lever to get water. The method where the container automatically fills up as the horse drinks is preferable.

> **Water you serve your horse should be water you'd serve yourself.**

Buckets and Tubs

Water can also be supplied in buckets, of course. Any bucket used should be of soft plastic for better wearing qualities; these are also less likely than metal or rigid plastic buckets to injure the horse should he tread or lie on them. Plastic buckets need only a simple daily scrub-out with an old dandy or water brush.

Particularly at night, a horse should be left with two rather widely spaced buckets of water instead of just one. If he fouls one with droppings, the other will still be clean for him to drink. If the two buckets are next to each other, the dropping will invariably go into both of them.

Troughs are satisfactory water sources for outdoor horses, but they require daily attention. Some people stock them with algae-eating carp to keep them clean (although this has been known to

> **Two buckets, side by side, can easily be fouled by a single pile.**

Water troughs are good sources of water for outdoor horses, so long as they are tended daily.

frighten the horses initially!), and, in any case, a regular clearing-out operation should take place to check for debris such as leaves and dead birds. During freezing weather, not only do you need to break the ice, but you should remove it as well as there are horses who are put off drinking, even when quite thirsty, by broken ice floating on the top of a trough. The supply should be checked twice daily to see that the trough is neither empty nor overflowing due to a malfunction of the ball-cock system, if it has one. All "moving parts," taps and other mechanisms should be securely covered with metal or wood to stop horses from fiddling with them.

Large plastic water tanks, sold by farm-supply stores and catalogs, are obviously good watering choices. Some rigid plastics may crack from freezing, strong sun and chewing or pawing by the horses, so troughs made of softer materials may be the better choice for durability. Lightweight tanks, such as these, have the advantage that they can be moved down one post each day so that the surrounding area does not become badly churned up and pocked, as often happens with fixed troughs.

A fixed trough can be a real advantage, however, if it is made to serve two fields by being set into the fence with access to animals on both sides. Do not set water containers in the corners of fields as this can cause escape problems if two or three horses are jostling to drink at the same time.

> A hose in winter wants treating as a pet; keep it dry and warm or you'll curse it yet.

Where running water and a proper trough are unavailable in a pasture or paddock, perfectly adequate watering sources can be provided by plastic garbage cans rammed into tires (this idea can also be adapted for buckets in stables) and tied by the handles to the fence posts. They can then be filled by hose from a nearby tap. Remember to keep the level high and to bring the hose indoors in frosty weather for if the water inside it freezes you are effectively without a hose until it thaws.

Water Au Naturel

Horses in fields are often left with a stagnant pond for water, a thoroughly unsuitable water source because of the toxic algae that can develop in still waters. These days, you have no assurance of the purity of streams and ponds either, so regular testing may be wise (consult your vet or county extension agent for laboratory recommendations).

In general, I question the safety of ponds as a horse-watering source and believe that they are better fenced off and left for wildlife. Horses and ponies can not only slip into them on unsafe approaches, but can wander onto the ice in winter with fatal results.

Supposedly, horses drinking from streams with sandy bottoms over a period of time may ingest a large quantity of sand, which collects in the bowel and causes recurrent colic. Consequently, if your turned-out horse takes his water from a natural source, hope that the bottom of his drinking hole is gravel or stone instead of sand. And, incidentally, if a horse consistently prefers muddy, seemingly unclean water to fresh, it could be a sign he is short of minerals in his diet.

Equine Digestion

Feeding

When horses are able to eat at their leisure, as when on a productive pasture, they tend to spend about sixteen hours a day nibbling grass and/or browsing on leaves from trees, shrubs and hedges. Vegetation such as this is their natural food, but it is fibrous and bulky, and they need to eat a lot of it to obtain sufficient nourishment. Therefore they have evolved to eat more or less continuously and always to have a little food passing through their digestive tracts.

This system is in direct contrast to that of their hunters in the wild. These carnivorous animals of the cat and dog families live on meat, a highly concentrated food, and have evolved to eat (when they can make a kill) one large meal all at once, often making it last them for several days. Carnivorous animals have, therefore, very large stomachs compared to herbivores, like horses, which have small stomachs and larger digestive tracts to cope with the continuous passage of fibrous foods.

Digestion starts in the mouth where the front teeth—the incisors—tear off grass and leaves and the grinding teeth at the back—the molars—crush and grind the food. The tongue manipulates it all, mixing it with saliva, which contains mild chemicals to prepare the food for the stronger digestive juices to come in the stomach.

The horse's stomach works best when two-thirds full, including both food and digestive juices. Once the food is mixed with digestive juices, it passes on down the digestive tract or intestine, which is a long, compartmentalized tube with muscular walls that push the food onwards in wavelike movements called peri-

---

**A hunter's stomach bulges with the kill;
a horse's stomach kills when it bulges.**

stalsis. In the gut, the food is mixed with other digestive juices and microscopic bacteria, which help process the food. Once extracted, the various nutrients are absorbed through the gut walls into the blood and lymph vessels and, after filtering by the liver, are then passed on to the various parts of the body needing them. The liver removes many harmful substances, changes them into harmless ones and excretes them again in the bile in a nonabsorbable form, helping to protect the body against poisoning. In cases where very potent poisons, such as ragwort, are eaten, the liver cannot cope and becomes seriously damaged, affecting its other functions and causing serious illness or death.

When horses take in more nutrients than required for their daily activities and growth, some excesses are excreted and others are stored in various "depots" for later use. Excess energy is never excreted, and the more that is stored, of course, the fatter the horse gets. Horses fed too little for their requirements obviously lose weight, as there is not only insufficient energy to store but insufficient energy to meet current needs. When a horse is starved, his body actually begins "burning" its own tissue, particularly muscle, for fuel (hence the descriptive phrase "skin and bones"), and the horse becomes emaciated.

If a horse becomes so thin that he is using up all of his body tissues, then obviously all the other requirements are affected; there is simply not enough fuel to keep the body going, and death can result. Conversely, when there is far too much food taken in for the body's requirements, such as when a horse is overfed and underworked or turned out for a rest on lush pasture, he will not only become fat but may also develop serious and sometimes fatal circulatory and digestive problems, such as colic and laminitis.

One of the essentials of life, third only to air and water, food is needed for

• production of body tissue such as muscle, skin, bone, hoof wall, etc.,

• maintaining the body's temperature at around 100.4 Fahrenheit,

• putting on condition (energy storage),

> **Blithely he chews his life away, not caring about proteins or carbos or what. While his owner plans his ration each day, horse eats solely to fill his gut.**

• providing fuel for vital, life-sustaining processes, such as heartbeat, hormone production and digestion, and work.

Feed Constituents

Feed constituents are varied and most feeds contain several types. The constituents are

- proteins,
- carbohydrates,
- fats,
- water,
- vitamins,
- minerals,
- trace elements,
- fiber.

Proteins contain the amino acids essential for the manufacture of body tissues, such as skin, muscles, organs and so on. Excess protein can be stored, although some is excreted by the kidneys. However, when it is stored it loses its tissue-building properties; therefore, a daily supply of protein is needed for growth and tissue repair. Apart from this "building" function of protein, it can also provide heat and energy, but only after a wasteful two-stage conversion process.

Most feeds fed to horses contain some protein, but while the traditional oats/timothy-hay regimen may provide enough of the essential amino acids to keep mature, moderately worked horses going, the same diet would fall short for other classes of horses, particularly growing youngsters. Soybean meal and alfalfa are the usual protein-rich ingredients in horse diets.

Carbohydrates are the starches and sugars in the diet. They produce energy and heat, and excess intake is stored as fat in the body. Grains, such as oats, corn and barley, are mainly carbohydrate, as are sweet feeds and other grain-based processed formulations. Carbohydrates are also found in grass, hay, sugar-beet pulp and molasses.

Fat is a normal component of cereal grains, with corn being the fattiest of them all. Though the natural herbivore diet contains nowhere near the ratio of fat found in the carnivore diet, it is possible to use supplemental fat—usually household cooking oil—as an extra energy source for hard-working horses. Race-horses, endurance horses, eventers, hunters and the like may reach the limits of their appetites or holding capacities before ingesting the amount of energy they need to do their work, and adding extra fat to their rations is an effective way of boosting energy without bulk. However, high-fat diets must also be high in choline and vitamin E to insure adequate chemical breakdown during digestion, and you should consult your vet or nutritionist for guidance in providing a properly balanced ration under these circumstances.

Fiber provides the essential bulk to a horse's diet, so necessary for giving him that comfortable feeling of satisfaction after a meal. Also referred to as "roughage," it is the woody part of vegetable matter and is of two types:

> **Pour on the energy by pouring on the oil.**

- cellulose, a form of digestible carbohydrate,

- lignin, the indigestible little "splinters" in horse manure, which physically break up the concentrated feed and allows the digestive juices to penetrate and do their job.

The intestine cannot work effectively if there is not enough bulk or fibrous material passing through it. Yet many horse caretakers seem to concentrate on the concentrates without much thought given to dietary fiber, which is present primarily in hay, straw and grain husks (better known as bran). Sweet feeds and pellets also contain some fiber, but even "complete" rations, which are supposed to supply all the roughage and concentrate a horse needs each day, do not furnish enough bulk for most horses, who very quickly become uncomfortably hungry and bored without hay to chew on. This results in mental problems and, in some cases, physical ones. If complete rations are fed, I recommend also feeding at least half the normal hay diet, with the majority given at night.

> **A bellyful of hay burns warmest on a winter's night.**

Vitamins, minerals and trace elements—called the **minor nutrients** not because they are of little consequence but because they comprise a tiny portion of the ration's total volume— are necessary for the processing of the other feed constituents and for maintaining critical body functions. Calcium and phosphorus and the proportional balance between the two are critical mineral concerns in horse diets, as is adequate intake of a dozen or so trace elements. The various essential vitamins are either present in generous amounts in the horse's natural grass diet or are manufactured within the horse's body, but as more horses must exist on diets with very little resemblance to nature's straight-grass menu, vitamin deficiencies are of growing concern.

Feed grains, grass and hay are the natural sources of these minor nutrients, but dietary levels are very much affected by

- mineral status of the soil in which the feeds are grown,

- conditions (droughty or too wet) of a particular growing season,

- environmental contaminants,

- feed processing,

- feed storage,

- age of feedstuffs.

When you see a lavishly advertised vitamin or mineral product, it's tempting to rush out and buy it, believing that it will give your horse a new zest for life and enable him to win the Kentucky Derby with no other help. In practice, however, indiscriminate feeding of these supplements is not only expensive but may also cause "overdosing" and imbalances. Most commercial concentrates are supplemented with a level of vitamins and minerals that will bring the diet, if fed as recommended, up to the standards recommended by the National Research Council's (NRC's) *Nutrient Requirements for Horses*. Bagged feeds are labelled with nutrient analyses, which, along with an analyses of hay samples, can be used by your vet or nutritionist to integrate the product into the horse's entire diet. As mentioned, I do feel it is worth the relatively economical fee of an expert to get reliable advice on what components, if any, should be supplemented, and whether a broad-spectrum product or simply a single, specialist one—maybe even a single vitamin or mineral—needs to be used to balance your horse's diet.

Owners who prefer to feed "straight" grains, such as oats, bran, barley, corn and so on, rather than commercial compounds can, unwittingly, be feeding diets which are seriously deficient or unbalanced. In these cases, a supplement might well be needed.

The more supplements, the worse.

Again, advice should be sought as no "ordinary" (professional or amateur) horse owner or manager has the detailed and, hopefully, up-to-date knowledge available to a qualified nutritionist.

Types of Feed

Having accepted that the horse's digestive system needs small amounts of food constantly passing along it, we have to consider what foods to use that will

- keep him feeling physically comfortable,

- provide his nutritional needs without weighing him down with unnecessary bulk,

- keep him in a fit condition to perform the work we ask of him.

Roughage is the most important "foundation" food for horses. The equine digestive system, as we have seen, cannot work effectively without a certain amount of fibrous bulk to give a feeling of satisfaction and fullness, to stimulate the movements of the digestive tract and to mix in with the concentrates to break them up and enable the digestive juices to penetrate and do their job.

Provided it is of reasonable in quality and available in adequate amounts, **grass** can provide all the nutrients necessary to support the activities of a mature, moderately worked pleasure horse. However, if harder work is demanded of the horse, the answer is not to put him on richer grazing. Remember that grass is very bulky, and the sheer weight of this type of food in the intestine is hardly conducive to strenuous work. Additionally, lush grazing, particularly nitrogen-rich spring grass, can cause serious disorders, such as laminitis and colic. The horse is unlikely to limit his intake himself, so we must do it for him by restricting his time at grass. Care should be taken when first introducing horses to this type of grazing, starting with half an hour daily and working up to probably no more than a couple of hours a day, depending on individual conditions.

Hay, the other roughage mainstay in horse diets, is simply green grass (primarily timothy, orchard grass, Bermuda grass and fescue) or legumes (most commonly alfalfa and clover), cut and dried to drop the moisture content to somewhere around 12 percent and thereby preserve the plant material for long-term use. Nutrient values vary tremendously among hays, in part due to the plant species—legumes are much higher in calcium than

---

> **A full belly brings forth every evil.**

grass hays, for example—and in part because of harvesting conditions—hay made from overmature plants, for instance, is much less nutritious than the same type of hay made from plants just coming into bloom. Good-quality hay alone can provide a quite adequate diet for horses who are in even moderately hard work.

Apart from being valuable food, hay offers another feeding advantage: it gives horses fulfillment for their innate urge to chew their way through the day. Munching on their roughage is a browsing activity equivalent to our reading books or watching television! If your horse is in good flesh or especially if he is overweight, you can still cater to his urge to chew without contributing to his girth by feeding him hay of lower nutrient content or giving him a reduced portion of higher quality hay in one of the special small-mesh hay nets which force horses to fiddle out only small amounts at a time and so take a longer time eating.

Another version of roughage feed is **"chop,"** which is hay and/or straw chopped up into small pieces about one inch long. This can usefully be mixed with the concentrate feed and, apart from forcing the horse to chew his food steadily and thoroughly, it aids digestion in the same way as hay. If you feed your horse his concentrate meal on return from exercise, it is a good idea to add some chop to the feed to prevent the horse from gobbling his meal if he has become especially hungry. Although feeding chop offers many digestive advantages, it is not common practice in the United States, and you will probably have to make special arrangements with a feed mill to cut roughage to your specifications if you wish to add chop to your horse's menu.

In years when local hay is poor or hard to get, some owners pay vast sums of money for hay shipped in from other regions or simply to grab up what little good hay is around. This is quite unnecessary and a false economy. Feeding a "complete" feed ration and offering clean oat straw to fulfill the horse's "chew" needs may well be cheaper. As straw is lower in food value than good hay, the shortfall will have to be made up with extra concentrates (consult your vet or nutritionist), but this is still cheaper than paying outrageous prices for hay.

> **When hay prices go sky high, the frugal feeder looks for substitutes.**

With all such feeds as hay or feed-straws, it is always cheaper to buy a crop "off the field" while it is still growing if you can, provided you stipulate that the purchase depends on the resulting quality being good. Buying at harvest time, or at least as early in the autumn as you can, is also a good idea. The price will invariably go up as winter passes, and you could be paying double the autumn price by spring or certainly by early summer. In fact, it normally works out cheaper to pay rent on storage space and buy a big load—often even getting a bank loan and paying interest on it—than to suffer high hay prices in the early half of the year.

Sugar-beet pulp, available in loose flakes or compressed into cubes, has been a successful roughage substitute for horses with hay allergies for years now, and the molasses-treated variety is liked by most. It also has the advantage of being high in calcium so can balance a typical old-fashioned high-phosphorus diet comprised of grain (oats, barley) and bran. Although research trials have shown that horses can, in fact, consume large quantities of dry pulp without harm, it is not something I would risk or recommend. Instead, soak the pulp, particularly the cubes, in at least six times its own volume of cold water for a good twenty-four hours before feeding. Soaking it in hot water may cause the pulp to ferment, leading to digestive problems.

Concentrates

We feed working horses concentrated foods to provide energy without bulk. A working horse has enough to do to carry or pull us around without being burdened with his own grass- or hay-filled gut, so we help him perform our work by giving him some of his fuel in more concentrated forms.

The energy-packed cereal grains used to feed horses include

> **The same measure of corn has twice the calories of oats.**

- **corn**, which contains the most calories (the unit used for measuring energy) by weight and by volume of any feed grain,

- **barley**, which is almost as energy-dense as corn but due to its dustiness and prickly husks is not particularly suitable for feeding "straight" to horses,

- **oats**, which provide less energy than most other grains but are traditionally the favored horse feed because of palatability and relative "safeness" in terms of overfeeding,

- **wheat**, **rye** and **other feed grains**, which are not normally fed "straight" to horses because of expense or palatability problems may be used as components in processed feeds.

Whole grains are often rolled, crushed or cracked when used as horse feed to break open their hard outer shells and make them more easily digested. Such processing does, however, contribute to vitamin loss and make the grain more apt to spoil. If you purchase whole grains, weight-to-volume is the most significant factor in assuring a good buy—the more pounds per bushel the better. The grains should be plump with plenty of body, not long and thin and nearly all husk.

The various grains fed to horses seem to have their detractors and as well as their proponents. In the United States, corn has a reputation for being a "hot" feed that puts horses on edge. In Britain, on the other hand, where corn (or maize, as it is called there) is not grown, oats are sometimes considered to be the "intoxicating" feed. Rather than arising from the feed grain itself, the adverse behavior is more likely the result of overfeeding of the concentrated energy source. Corn is particularly easy to overfeed because of its great energy density. Some animals become really silly when fed too much grain and are dangerous if under-exercised. As mentioned earlier, many working horses can do quite nicely on a diet of good hay alone, so rather than blame a particular type of grain for a horse's as-high-as-a-kite behavior, perhaps you might try cutting way back on concentrates of any type and feeding more hay to see if you can get better behavior without a serious loss of condition.

Pelleted feeds contain many finely ground ingredients bound together, usually in a molasses base, and shaped into various-sized pellets, whereas those same ingredients are either whole or only slightly processed in **sweet feeds** (also called **textured feeds**) but are again bound together with molasses. A good product will be properly balanced in all the essential nutrients, and you will probably get better results than feeding "straights" (i.e. separate ingredients such as oats or corn with bran) and perhaps an expensive supplement which takes your fancy because of an eye-catching advertisement in a horse magazine! The supplement itself may well be a superb product but not right for your particular ration or horse. With commercial feeds, you simply have to weigh out the correct amount, and you should then have no problems about dietary balance.

A commonly given reason for not using processed feeds is "I like to see what I'm feeding." Actually, although with such feeds as oats and barley, you know that they are oats and barley you still cannot see what you are feeding because unless you have them

---

**So you know what you're feeding
when you give straight grain?
Then show me the sack of oats or corn
with a nutrient analysis on the label.**

analyzed you do not know exactly what is in them. With pellets and sweet feeds at least the analysis is on the bag—and I have yet to come across a sack of oats with that information on it. It should also be noted that all feed grains are deficient in an important protein constituent—lysine—so advice should be sought with regard to supplying this essential nutrient in a grain-only concentrate ration.

This does not mean that I am against feeding straight grains, but I am against feeding an ingredient of unknown nutrient content. It's advisable that, whatever ingredients you want to feed, to enlist the professional help of a veterinarian or an equine nutritionist/management consultant in getting your horse's diet formulated and the ingredients (including the hay) analyzed. It will be more economical in the long run and more effective from your horse's point of view.

Although commercial mixes from reliable suppliers are properly balanced, many people still find it hard not to tinker with their horses' diets, adding a bit of this and a bit of that in the form of other ingredients which have a significant feed value and which, inevitably, throw the diet out of balance. You can add things like carrots, apples, molasses, honey and so on, if you wish, without upsetting the nutritional apple cart, but additional carbohydrates, such as oats, barley, flaked corn or mixed brands of pellets or sweet feed, make nonsense of the carefully balanced diet provided by the manufacturers of good commercial products. The same goes for adding "goodies" to the "complete" feeds which are in themselves balanced. Feed supplements, too, should not be added to already-balanced feeds without truly expert advice (from a nutritionist or vet), even broad-spectrum (general) ones as they will probably be superfluous and maybe disadvantageous or even dangerous.

> **An extra pinch of this and scoop of that, make nonsense of the most scientific mix.**

"Invalid" Feeds

If you are the sort who likes to give your horse a special ration after a particularly exhausting work or competition, during recuperation from illness or just because the weather is being especially unpleasant, you're likely to have served up a bran mash or two in your time. **Bran**, a processed form of the outer, fibrous husk of wheat grains, has for generations been a valued feed for horses, used to pad out the concentrate ration and make the ubiquitous bran mash which we have been told by our predecessors is a valuable, easily digested, laxative feed for a tired or sick horse.

In fact, bran is, for a number of reasons, a poor choice as a horse feed, whether used for healthy animals or invalids:

• Bran mashes are not easily digested feeds suitable for tired or sick horses. Bran's laxative effect results from the gut's natural reaction an undigestible burden—it tries to get rid of it as quickly as possible. The last thing a tired or sick horse needs is a difficult-to- digest feed and a gut in spasm.

• Bran mashes are also unappetizing, as confirmed by the advice to add a handful of salt or oats to make it more acceptable, so again they are not the sort of feed you would want to give a horse whose appetite needs stimulating.

• Bran can create a dietary imbalance between phosphorous and calcium. Phosphorous-rich itself, bran contains a substance which blocks the absorption of calcium from other foods. The phosphorous excess resulting from frequent bran intake can cause brittle, porous and enlarged bones prone to fracture and other problems.

• Bran is an expensive feed, especially considering how little it contributes to horses' nutrient needs. Good bran—broad flakes and plenty of flour—is now very hard to get and even more expensive than the poorer sort resembling sawdust. So save money and don't bother too much about using bran.

> **A sick horse fed bran today may be a sicker horse tomorrow.**

If you feel that you must use a little bran to improve the texture of a feed or as a useful base for mixing in medicine, make sure it is a little—no more than one part bran to six parts concentrates (by weight, not volume).

Now, what will help an ailing horse (or perk up the spirits of his caretaker on a dismal day) if a bran mash is a faulty nutritional choice? Try the following feeding suggestions for equine "invalids" and other horses with special needs, and you'll be bolstering their well-being rather than hindering it:

• Use chop (described earlier) to add bulk to the concentrate portion of the ration.

• If the horse needs a laxative, consult with your veterinarian about the entire diet, feeding regime and the horse's digestive health. An inadequate supply of water and overly coarse hay are the most common causes of constipation, and in addition to correcting these two contributors to the problem, if you can allow the horse access to grass, his troubles will likely be over.

• Substitute "false" feeds of chop, soaked sugar-beet pulp, cut grass (although not fine lawn clippings which can ferment and cause serious colic) and/or thinly sliced roots such as carrots for his regular concentrates during "down times" due to incapacity or training interruptions. Add a single handful of his normal concentrate feed to keep the digestive bacteria going until he's back at work and back on full feed again.

• Cooked, flaked barley can serve as a high-calorie ration for sick or thin horses (or simply a treat for a hard-worked companion). To make it, place the grain in a large sieve and put the sieve over a large pan of boiling water. The steam rising through the grains will cook and soften them. Stir the grains regularly until they are thoroughly soft. As far more harm can come from slightly overfeeding a horse than slightly underfeeding him, be sure the amount of barley used does not exceed the amount, by weight, of concentrate in the everyday ration.

Energy Requirements

What "grade" of feed to give can also create problems. In the past we have tended to gauge food on its protein content. Racehorse mixes, for instance, are invariably around 14 percent protein, while rations for pleasure horses are 11 or 12 percent. It is more accurate nowadays to go by the energy content of the product, as we now know that horses need less protein, in general, than was previously believed. A 10 percent protein ration is now considered sufficient for most classes of mature horses, except broodmares, and only foals and youngstock actually require the sixteen-percent formulations for growth.

Energy is the nutrient that fuels horses' daily activities, so work level and growth are the two factors that determine the carbohydrate requirement of the ration. Most brand-name horse feeds now come in different formulations for different classes of horses, with energy and protein levels adjusted to the needs of moderately worked pleasure horses, hard-working performance horses, growing youngstock and broodmares.

Your "straights," such as oats, barley and corn, plus your hay and other roughage don't come with such neat use guidelines,

> **Excess protein is a costly way
> to make your horse fat;
> simple carbohydrates will do the trick
> at half the cost.**

but you can find out the actual levels of digestible energy (DE) in each foodstuff by having samples analyzed in a laboratory recommended by your vet or a nutritionist or you can refer to standard tables of nutrient values of different feeds to get a ballpark estimate.

The following general guidelines will also help you determine the relative energy density of horse feeds:

• Fats are the most concentrated energy sources, followed by the carbohydrate-rich grains.

• The greater the fiber content of a feedstuff, the lower the energy value; therefore more mature grass/hay has fewer calories per pound than "pre-bloom" grass/hay, and grain with a lot of husk or chaff provides less energy per volume measure than clean, plump, chaffless grain.

• Legume hays (alfalfa and clover) have more calories per pound than grass hays when both are harvested at the same stage of maturity.

• The higher the water content of the feed, the lower its per-pound calorie count.

You do need to know the energy content and nutritional balance of the entire diet if you are to feed both concentrates and roughages accurately. Of course, it is possible to work without this information, using just the horse's condition as a guide, but it may result in your feeding, for example, small portions of a high-energy feed because the horse is jumping all over the place or going down with laminitis, but then he ends up being hungry, uncomfortable and prone to wood-chewing and other vices because of a never-satisfied urge to fill his gut. If you are aware of the calorie count of various feeds, you can create a diet of lower-energy roughage and concentrate to keep the horse's appetite satisfied without pumping him overfull of dangerous energy.

This is where commercial feeds come into their own. Not only are they correctly balanced in regards to vitamins, minerals, trace elements, fats and proteins but you can find out for certain what the energy level is and what class of horse the mix is geared to. The diet may need adjusting anyway, but the adjustments will be far smaller if you start out with certain knowledge of what you are feeding rather than guessing the energy levels of "straights"—or waiting for the horse to tell you by his behavior and condition.

Determining Quantity

The most reliable way to calculate how much feed to give a horse is to use his bodyweight as a guide; this is done quite simply by using one of the special tape measures designed for the purpose (available from some nutritionists, feed firms and veterinary practices). These save a lot of calculating and messing about—no need to trek to the nearest scale or work out from the results how much total food to give. The tapes are graduated so that you simply read off the horse's measurement round the girth, and his weight and consequent daily food requirement.

Alternatively, you can measure round the horse's girth just behind the withers, making sure the binder twine, tape measure or whatever you are using, is straight and that you take the measurement at the end of one of the horse's "out" breaths. Then, using the tables in Appendix 3, you can estimate the horse's or pony's weight and from there go on to calculate how much—by weight—his total daily food intake needs to be.

> **First weigh the horse, then weigh the feed.**

Moderately active mature horses and some ponies will usually require two pounds of feed per one hundred pounds of bodyweight to maintain their current condition. In other words, your 1200 pound horse will need and want to eat a combined total of 24 pounds of hay and grass and concentrates daily to satisfy his maintenance requirements. Ponies and colder-blooded horses who easily get fat should receive less, particularly of concentrates. Lactating broodmares, growing youngstock and adults in particularly strenuous work may need to consume more than the theoretical two pounds per hundredweight—if they have the time and space to fit it in. It is more accurate, of course, to weigh your animal on a scale, but if you haven't access to one, you'll find the above method to be a very good substitute.

Just about any animal should be fed so that you cannot actually see its ribs but can feel them quite easily. From this starting point, you can adjust the diet to keep the animal in good condition, neither too fat nor too thin. Physical fitness usually means getting rid of excess fat and building up muscle in its place. Those animals doing hard work who are naturally lean may just show the last two pairs of ribs, but there is no excuse for any more showing. The horse's type as well as his individual tendencies should also be considered. For example, a 15-hand Quarter Horse may look fat to the naked eye compared with a 15-hand Arabian but both may be in good condition for their types and work.

How to split the total ration between concentrates and roughage for horses on a conventional diet (as opposed to one of the forage-only regimes) depends on the work being done. For a horse doing about two hours a day of moderately active hacking (mostly walking and trotting with a bit of cantering and jumping), a suggested split, by weight, is two-thirds roughage and one-third concentrates. For the 1,200-pound horse mentioned above, this would mean sixteen pounds of hay and eight pounds of grain. If you give the horse free-choice hay, you will probably find that he splits it this way himself.

If you're not sure about how much hay to feed a new horse, you can start out by giving him so much for the evening feeding that he still has some left in the morning. Weigh the leftovers, and deduct the figure from the total amount you left him the night before. For his next night's ration, give him four to five pounds less than the amount you calculated he ate the previous night. This portion should be enough to leave him satisfied and not wanting to eat his bedding yet not too "full" in the morning to exercise first thing. When you know how much hay your horse eats in a twenty-four-hour period, you may well discover that this amount deducted from the total feed-bodyweight calculation results in the amount of concentrates you have to feed to maintain his condition. This is what I have found in practice.

It will always be a case of "the eye of the master making the horse fat." Some horses are much better doers than others, requiring less food to keep in good condition than the naturally leaner sort who may never look as rounded as their colleagues yet may be perfectly all right in their own way.

> **Never more pounds of concentrate feed than pounds of roughage to a working steed.**

Judging Quality

From a practical point of view, there are certain steps you can take to insure that the feed you purchase is of reasonable quality. Although this in itself will not confirm its actual feeding value, you can be assured that poorly harvested and carelessly stored feeds will be lower in at least some essential nutrients than well-tended provender. When you go to buy feeds for your horse, put them through the following "tests":

• First, take a sniff of the roughage or grain. Any feed that smells unpleasant—sour, musty or dirty—should be turned down. Good hay, in particular, is usually noted for its "nose" or pleasant, sweet aroma. Concentrates, too, should have a slightly sweet odor, especially sweet feeds with molasses as an ingredient. If your whiff makes you cough, it's likely that the feed is moldy and will be even worse for your horse.

• Taste grains such as oats and corn; they should be sweet and starchy tasting. Highly processed feed, such as pellets, usually taste horrible to us, so use their smell and appearance as a guide to their quality. They should be hard and dry with no sour smell. If soft and damp, refuse them.

• Look for clumping of concentrates, especially with an off color to the clumps. Although molasses-rich sweet feeds normally cling together, particularly in subfreezing weather, all other grains and pelleted feeds should be free of congealed lumps and pour freely from the container. If they aren't, moisture damage and/or molds are present.

• Check hay for springiness and heft. Bales that are exceptionally "fluffy" and light are "clean" but often contain aged hay of low nutrient content, which may be useful for providing low-calorie chew food for overweight horses. Hard, heavy, unyielding bales are usually blocks of musty or moldy hay that is not only unpalatable but outright unhealthy for horses. Quality hay has the feel in between these two extremes—relatively soft and yielding but hefty enough to promise some solid nutrition.

In appearance, hay should be greenish to golden, with closed seed heads. If the seed heads are open, it has obviously "gone to seed," and its feeding value is much lower than it would have been if harvested a week or so earlier. If the hay is dull or stemmy rather than leafy, brassy or washy yellow or brownish and smells either musty or sour—maybe even with visible white or black mold on it and giving off clouds of dust when shaken out—it is not even fit for bedding, although you could perhaps use it (after receiving a very substantial discount from the supplier) for mulching your garden. This is all such hay is fit for.

When you open a bale of hay it should spring apart rather than stay where it is or simply drop lifelessly apart, and the hay should be easy to shake out with no sign of dust. Grass hay should feel and look glossy and smooth and have a sweet, appetizing smell. Alfalfa and clover hays should have fine stems and lots of leaves. Hay which smells like tobacco is often thought to be good, but in fact it is slightly "mowburnt," or overheated during storage, and will not be of particularly high feeding value. It may even be harmful, although many horses love it just as many humans love cigarettes!

Research work in Scotland has shown that samples of hay given to expert horsemen for quality judging were rated according to traditional methods and opinions. When each sample was compared with the actual laboratory analysis, it turned out that the most desirable samples from the horsemen's points of view often had poor feed value compared with other samples they had

There's more to good hay than meets the eye or tickles the nose.

downgraded. So judging hay on tangible qualities alone should, perhaps, be regarded as no more than a general guide to what not to buy—that is, buy nothing dirty, moldy, dusty or sour/musty smelling. Anything else, get analyzed so you'll know exactly what you are feeding. Really good dealers may well have nutrient analyses of various lots of hay all ready for you to examine before purchase.

Straw, whether intended for feeding or bedding, should be subject to the same sight-and-smell tests as hay. Moldy straw is every bit as dangerous to a horse's health due to spores that can be inhaled or ingested. If you intend to feed the straw rather than use it as bedding, get it analyzed for nutrient content so you can balanced the rest of the ration around it.

As a working owner, you might find it difficult to arrange deliveries of your feedstuffs and bedding. Usually someone has to sign for a shipment, which usually arrives during the workday. This could mean that you have to pick up your own feed, inconvenient though this is. You may be able to have a family member of acquaintance accept your delivery, but unfortunately this means you cannot check the quality of your shipment before signing, which is highly desirable—particularly in the case of a supplier you have never dealt with before.

Some of the less reputable dealers keep their best hay and straw for farmers and big owners, palming off the substandard stuff to horse owners whom they think don't know any better and will pay through the nose for almost anything. Learn to judge quality, therefore; ask questions about analysis and religiously send or take back any feed which is no good. When you are able to be present for your own deliveries, undo the sacks (except possibly those containing brand-name pellets or sweet feeds) and check the quality before signing.

> **Receive before you write, and write before you pay.**

The Importance of Consistency

We are constantly told never to make sudden changes in feeding, but it is not usually stressed that this applies to every single feed, not merely to the diet as a whole. Because of the sensitive nature of the horse's digestive system and the fact that, in nature, he eats a little of the same ingredients all the time, we should mimic this system and feed the same ingredients at every feeding, varying only the amounts given. For instance, if your horse is suddenly thrown out of work, your instinct should be to drastically cut down, or cut out, his concentrates, particularly if he is to be stallbound. Proceed by cutting concentrates in half, then half again and so on until the horse is getting no more than a single handful at each feeding. At the same time you're decreasing the concentrates, increase by equal amounts (by weight) the quantities of other ingredients, such as chop, sugar-beet pulp, cut grass, grated carrots and so on.

The point is that whatever ingredients you use must be those he is already used to, so always use some of each ingredient in his diet at each feeding. The reason for this is that the horse largely digests his food by means of microscopic bacteria and protozoa in his intestines. These microorganisms, as they are known, actually digest the horse's food for him, using it as their own food, and they, too, need a consistent, reliable diet. If they don't get it, they die off and are not available when more of "their" type of food comes along, at least not in sufficient numbers to do a good job, so the horse suffers either incomplete digestion, indigestion or actual colic. Apart from being bad management, this is also wasteful. The microorganisms will start dying off in as little as four hours if an inconsistent diet fails to provide "their" food.

For this reason, also, new ingredients must be introduced gradually so that the population of appropriate microorganisms has a chance to build up to sufficient numbers to digest them. Do not, for example, feed pellets for breakfast, sweet feed for lunch, plain oats for supper and so on. Do not feed a weekly bran mash for the same reason (among others already mentioned). Do not change abruptly from one batch of the feed to a new lot but gradually mix a little of the new with the old until you eventually change over. This applies to each fresh batch of hay, pellets, sweet feed, chop or "straights." It is easy to arrange once you get used to operating on this principle, and it is so important to your horse's digestive system and well-being.

When to Feed

It is never a good idea to work a horse immediately after a feed because of the digestive and respiratory problems this can cause. The lungs and stomach lie right next to one another, separated only by a strong but thin sheet of muscle called the diaphragm. During work, the lungs have to expand and the heart has to work more than during rest. If they are hampered by a neighboring full stomach, their action could be interfered with—as could that of the stomach by the expanding lungs and rapidly beating heart. With free-choice supplies of hay, however, horses rarely gorge themselves as do those who are left for long periods without food.

If you arrange your schedule so that your horse will have finished his hay an hour or two before you intend to work him, you will avoid such problems. It's especially important when you

> **Feed well the wee beasties in your horse's gut, for they are what feed him well.**

> **Work not thy horse on a stomach too full, nor one too empty.**

want to exercise him in the early mornings before going to work. If his evening meal contains enough hay to last him until the small hours, you can safely take him out without his breakfast, knowing he has not had time to become particularly hungry. By following this sort of feeding and exercise plan, you won't have to work him straight after a feeding or wait for him to digest a meal before getting on with your ride. (Nevertheless, it is always wise to "walk the first mile out and the last mile home," as the old adage goes.)

In the morning, exercise the horse first, then give him some hay to nibble on for a short time while you put his tack away. On return, give him his concentrate feed, if appropriate, and finally leave him with a full supply of hay to eat and digest in peace while you go off to earn the money to buy him some more! Alternatively, you could give him his concentrate feed, stock up his field shelter with hay while he is eating his grain, and then turn him into the paddock or stable to eat his hay ration while you are at work. These practices save you a lot of time and avoid working the horse on a full stomach.

Communal Feeding Concerns

Problems over routine can arise in communal stables. It may be necessary for individual owners to vary their routines so that incompatible grazing companions are not turned out together for the sake of avoiding injuries. Also, horses in communal stables tend to be brought to and from the paddocks and in and

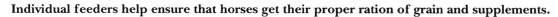

Individual feeders help ensure that horses get their proper ration of grain and supplements.

out from exercise at widely varying times, according to their owners' schedules. This sometimes worries owners who prefer to feed not only at regular times (usually given as one of the golden rules of feeding) but also at the same time as other horses, to prevent any "left out" feelings. It is true that, if horses are fed all at the same time and at regular hours, they do indeed come to expect it, and can create havoc if their routine is broken or some are left out, making slaves of their owners.

Think what happens, however, to horses regularly taken away to shows and other activities. Their routine is invariably broken to some extent, and horses in the stable areas are certainly not fed all at the same time. Police horses are another example; these are genuine working animals who have to adapt to work circumstances and requirements. They return to the stables at varying hours throughout the day and night and are fed as and when it is convenient, within reason. Some horses will be at home and will already have been fed when the latecomers arrive; they do not kick up a fuss when the latter are fed, partly because they are used to this irregular pattern but partly also because they have already had their own feed and are not hungry.

The "secret" of being able to feed horses at different times in the same stable without problems, I have found, is not letting any of the animals get really hungry. The same goes for owners who work irregular shifts and cannot arrange identical feed times every day for their horses. In any of these cases, leave the horse enough hay or other roughage to keep him occupied and prevent hunger and the actual time of concentrate feeding is not that important, within an hour or so.

I have recommended more than once that it is a good idea to have the field shelter stocked up with hay to keep the horses happy and occupied when the grass is not up to much. In communal stables, again, it may not be easy at first try to organize this. There is no point in one owner putting out hay for her horse if it is going to be eaten by all the others whose owners have not done so. However, as in the case of deworming, an informal meeting can be called to suggest that all owners contribute a certain amount of money or hay every week to a "field hay" stock, the amounts varying according to their horses' appetites. Then hay can safely be put out for all the horses. This will not cost any more on top of normal feed costs, for the horses will eat that much less at other times, probably spending their stabled hours resting more.

As ever, mutual common sense and cooperation can only do but good, and everyone will benefit, particularly the horses.

It is obviously not possible to control a horse's diet absolutely minutely when he is on grass, but in practice this really is not necessary. And one has to be realistic in such matters and not develop a fetish about feeding. To keep a horse away from grass—his natural food—simply because one does not know the exact analysis of every mouthful would plainly be quite ridiculous.

Grass and herbs, in particular, contain many nutrients that a horse may well not get in an artificial diet except by the possible inclusion of expensive feed supplements. Pasture is also one of the cheapest feeds you can give your horse. During spring, summer and autumn, it can provide a valuable and much appreciated element in his diet. If the grass is reasonably well cared for and the horse is doing even moderate work—easily an hour or two of light hacking daily—it could well form all or most of his diet.

Looking After Your Pasture

Sadly, most horse paddocks are dreadfully neglected. They are overgrazed and littered with droppings. The grass in the lavatory areas—horses designate such areas in their paddocks—

This is an excellent example of good pasture.

Pasture Maintenance

grows long and rank as the horses will not graze there, while the grazing areas can become as bald as a billiard table.

To be productive, land and grass need some care, including

• drainage and/or erosion control (wet land is cold and oxygen starved and usually seethes with flies in summer, while erosion pollutes the air and surrounding waterways and denudes your land of nutrient-rich topsoil),

• weed control (inedible and harmful vegetation must be removed in the interests of greater productivity for the land and greater safety for your horses, whether you use sprays or hand labor),

• seeding/reseeding (a healthy grass cover will not only provide more food for your horses but will reduce erosion and weed infestations as well),

• fertilizing and liming (you have to feed your land to make pasture a valuable feed source for horses),

• regular mowing during growing season (a well-tended pasture is not only more attractive, it produces more palatable grass and fewer weeds than ones left ragged and gone to seed),

• manure removal (aside from the health benefits to the horses grazing upon the land, frequent manure removal keeps more of your pasture in edible "lawns" rather than contaminated—from the horse's perspective—"roughs" suitable only for dropping more manure).

> There's no better medicine—nor cheaper feed— than the horses' favorite, Dr. Green.

Soil type varies widely, not only in different parts of the country but from field to field in some localities, and in order manage your pastures well, in terms of fertilizing, liming and seeding, you need to know your soil. Expert analysis by a management consultant, your county extension agent or a fertilizer salesman will reveal the condition of your land and what you need to do to make it more productive. Extension soil tests cost only a few dollars, and fertilizer and seed companies may do free analyses if you buy their products.

Seeding mixtures will vary, depending on the soil and climate in your area, but it is worthwhile stressing to whoever is helping you that the field is for horses, not cattle. Nitrogen-rich varieties and nitrogen fertilizers producing a quick flush of rich grass are not suitable for horses and can cause digestive and circulatory troubles.

Fertilizing your land with cattle manure seems to disguise the smell of horse droppings on paddocks and so brings back into use areas which horses may previously have been avoiding. Spreading cattle manure thickly in the autumn would seem to be a good idea for this reason alone (provided the parasite problem can be sorted out), apart from the valuable organic fertilizer it affords. Old-fashioned farmstead manure comprised of droppings, urine and straw is not always available these days, however, due to the modern tendency to keep the animals on unbedded feedlots. The resultant slurry is far too rich and lacking in humus to be safe to put on horse paddocks unless you are taking a hay crop first before grazing the horses on the new grass as it is too high in nitrogen. For these reasons, it is as well to consult an equine-management specialist rather than a farm/cattle orientated person who may not understand horses' needs.

Rotation

When the vegetation is sorted out, a rotation will have to be devised to keep the pasture in good shape. If you can manage it, divide your land into at least two sections with temporary electric fencing—three or more sections are even better—so each division can be used, treated and rested in turn. After horses have grazed the land for three or four weeks (not months, as is often the case), you may notice it is taking on a patchy appearance, with some areas growing long and others remaining short. That is the time to move the horses on to the next rotation strip and to cut the long grass down and harrow the field to aerate it and pull out dead grass and roots. Apply any fertilizer recommended and finally rest. Continue this rotation with the other division(s).

Even when you are renting pasture land for as short a time as one summer, you will find that a little time and money spent on getting it in shape will pay dividends in an improved grass crop for the nutrition and pleasure of your animals. Those on ample and suitable grazing rarely get into trouble by trying to jump out in search of greener pastures, by experimenting with poisonous plants or by stirring up a fracas among the other horses due to boredom or hunger. It is cheaper to buy fertilizer to improve grass than to buy extra feed—and even the hardest working and fittest horses (including racehorses) benefit from time spent at grass, even an hour or so providing a welcome mental and physical break from the usual work/stable/hard-feed routine.

> **Take care of your pasture, and it will take care of your horses.**

Doing the Jobs

Getting the work done may not be easy, but the regular chores can be accomplished with the help of family, friends or fellow "commune" owners. Such tasks as cutting the long grass can be done by riding lawn mowers so long as the terrain isn't too daunting and you do it before the grass gets too heavy (if you use a mower with a grass catcher, scatter the clipping on over-grazed areas to rot down there and add valuable nutrients, but keep horses away from the clippings for several days). On uneven terrain you can even try cutting the grass by scythe if you can get hold of one these days—they are not that difficult to use once you get the knack. Of course, a tractor-drawn agricultural mower is best, as it makes light work of the job.

Droppings can be picked up by hand on a weekly basis; fertilizer can be spread from the back of a truck, horse-drawn trailer, van or hatchback car on a still day; and a sensible horse can easily be rigged up cheaply and taught to pull a chain harrow over the field. Probably the only contract labor you will have to pay for in maintaining your pasture is manure spreading and any soil-conservation measures you choose to employ.

When you have grass to spare, there is no reason why you cannot be as canny as, in my experience, most farmers are and get them to pay for your grazing by offering to let them run some cattle on your land at cut-rate prices. (Determine the prevailing rate by perusing advertisements for grazing in the local farming press or contacting several local farmers.) If you succeed in getting a taker, you can put the rent money into your kitty budget to pay for the fertilizer, a secondhand chain harrow, and so forth. Or perhaps you can bypass the cash and trade the grazing for regular pasture mowing or fence repairs.

Cattle should be polled (hornless) as most are these days, and free from diseases, such as ringworm. This last topic should be discussed with your veterinarian, who can give you details of cattle diseases that might affect your horses.

> **And why can't the horse help care for his own pasture?**

Parasite Control

It is no longer recommended to harrow pastures for the purpose of scattering droppings even within the lavatory areas, as this has been found to spread the eggs and resultant larvae rather than exposing them to the sun and air to be desiccated. Information is also beginning to emerge which suggests that it might not be so beneficial as has been believed up to now to graze cattle on horse pastures. The cattle do eat off the long grass in the horses' lavatory areas (these do not offend the cattle) and drop their own much-needed manure on the horses' grazing areas (which in turn does not bother the horses). Horse parasites taken in by the cattle will die off in an unnatural host and vice versa, but it seems that there are some parasites which are common to both species and that cattle can, therefore, actually infect a paddock with parasites not previously there, which can infect the horses in turn. Your veterinarian should be able to keep you up to date on these matters and may be able to recommend a suitable anthelmintic (worm medicine) to cover all bases.

Picking up the droppings from paddocks will not only add to the size and value of your manure heap but can also significantly reduce the risk of worm infection if the task is done at least every three days. Manure removal is particularly beneficial for small or overcrowded fields sustaining one or more horses per acre. However, if the horses are dewormed at regular six-weeks intervals throughout the year, the numbers of eggs and larvae dropped on the land should be negligible.

The drug ivermectin (marketed as Eqvalan through veterinarians and Zimecterin over the counter) kills the immature, larval forms of almost all equine parasites during the parts of their life cycles when they are still circulating in the blood vessels and it disables the mature forms. Therefore, you can deworm with ivermectin less often than with dewormers which do not kill arterial stages of worms. However, while it kills intestinal parasites (including bloodworms, the most dangerous), skin parasites (such as those responsible for "summer sore"), bots and lungworms, it does not kill tapeworms, which are becoming more significant in horse populations. The drug pyrantel, administered at twice the dosage recommended on the label, does kill these, however, plus intestinal parasites but not bots and the skin parasites.

To keep the infestation of your paddocks and horses down to a minimum and to be sure you are deworming your horse frequently enough with the right drugs for the worms he has, you can ask your veterinarian to carry out fecal tests and perhaps blood tests, as well, to find out what parasites are present and then to work out an effective treatment and prevention program for your circumstances. Sometimes the anthelmintic needs changing; sometimes the dose level and timing require adjustment. For instance, to kill bots you need to deworm with a boticide (a drug which kills bots) after the first frost of the autumn or winter. The frost will kill the adult, egg-laying females, and the subsequent treatment will kill the immature bot larvae that otherwise would spend the next nine or ten months attached to the lining of your horse's stomach. If every horse owner in the country followed this procedure just one fall, bots would become extinct! (Unless they fly in from overseas the next spring.)

If you are in the unfortunate but common situation of keeping your horse at an establishment where the other owners will not agree to join in a proper deworming program and treat all horses

> **At the same time you lighten your horse's parasite load, you'll lighten your feed bill.**

at the same time, you can at least keep your own horse's infestation levels down reasonably by using ivermectin most of the time to remove immature and mature parasites, with occasional pyrantel treatments to deal with tapeworms, as required, according to your vet's advice. There is also a recently released pyrantel dewormer that is designed to be fed daily and thereby cause a continuous kill of immature as well as mature parasites. Horses receiving this treatment are protected regardless of the parasite burdens of their pasture mates. At present (1993) there is no reported resistance among equine parasites to either ivermectin or pyrantel.

As mentioned previously, all horses and ponies using the field must be dewormed at the same time—and every time—if infection is to be controlled. This goes for any donkeys, too. With the latter there is still the risk of lungworm being passed on, so discuss matters with your vet if this is your situation. It is, of course, very difficult to care properly for land that is not your own in arrangements where you are not "The Boss." If you keep your horse at a communal do-it-yourself stable, with or without a caring manager/proprietor on hand, it is well worthwhile getting all the other owners together and making sure they all realize the advantages of removing horse droppings from the field and, even more important, of having all of the horses dewormed at the same time.

> **In common pasture infection lies:**
> **My horse**
> **even treated**
> **is at the mercy**
> **of yours**
> **full of worms.**

Grooming and Blanketing

Grooming is a time-consuming task that can be quite hard work for the inexperienced and unfit. It is certainly necessary, not only because it aids good health and condition but also because it is no pleasure to ride or drive a dirty horse. It is also bad for the reputation of horsepeople everywhere for some of their number to be seen out with unkempt animals.

Why Groom?

The horse's skin, like that of other animals, is continually shedding dead scales from its outer layer, which forms the dandruff seen in an ungroomed horse's coat. Skin, like everything else, has a limited life span and is continually being shed and replaced throughout the year. The skin also produces natural oils to lubricate itself and the coat hairs and to give some protection against wet weather and, to a much lesser extent, cold. The coat hairs grow out of follicles in the skin, and they, too, are being shed constantly throughout the year, although the main times of shedding are spring and autumn.

The amount of grooming a horse receives depends not only on how much time his owner has but on how he is kept and what work he is doing. A fit, stabled horse in fairly hard work will probably get roughly an hour's grooming a day. If you put tack or harness on top of dried sweat or mud, it can easily rub a sore place, which may mean the horse cannot be worked normally until it has healed. Therefore, even if pushed for time, you should brush away mud and dried sweat in areas that will be in contact with tack before you exercise the horse.

When done sympathetically—gently where necessary, on sensitive areas like the head and belly, and firmly where appropriate, such as the long strokes used on the neck, trunk and quarters of the horse—the grooming process

- helps build a bond between horse and handler,

- stimulates the skin and removes dirt, excess grease and dead skin,

- enables the handler to spot any skin irregularities, such as lumps, wounds, rashes, unusual hair loss and soreness, either visually, by feel or by noticing the horse's responses to being groomed,

- reveals any external parasites, such as ticks and lice, that may not be apparent in a dirty coat.

> **One unkempt horse tars the whole neighborhood of conscientious keepers.**

Although grooming is an important task, there may well be days when you simply haven't the time to give your stabled horse a thorough going over. What should be done every day is the sponging of eyes, nostrils, lips, sheath, udder and dock, including the underside of the tail itself which is often forgotten. And certainly the feet need to be picked out and the shoes checked twice daily.

Horses at grass are not commonly body brushed, anyway, but should get a basic daily check in which you run your hands carefully over every inch of the horse to detect any irregularities.

Timesaving Techniques and Equipment

When body brushing, which is the main part of the full grooming process, many people use much more strength and energy than necessary because they are doing it incorrectly. You need to save energy otherwise you may not have enough to do the job effectively, especially if you are grooming more than one horse. Hold the body brush with a stiff arm that's slightly bent at the elbow. Then lean your weight on the arm and so against the horse to push the bristles through the coat, rather than using your arm, shoulder and back muscles to push the brush. You will find this much less tiring and just as effective.

For real speed, however, try a trick I developed some years ago. Get yourself a tough pair of leather chaps and two of the hand-held metal curry combs, the type with a fabric or leather band across the back for you to slip your hand into rather than the kind with a wooden handle extending from it. Use leather thongs or bailer twine to fasten these curry combs to the tops of the thighs of the chaps by passing the thread (or whatever you are using) along the grooves between the metal teeth and into holes punched in the chaps and tieing them together firmly inside the chaps. Secure both ends of the curry comb to the chaps so they are firmly fixed.

Now take a body brush in each hand. Work quickly all over the horse giving long firm strokes with alternate hands, as you normally do with only one hand. When you want to clean the brushes, as you should every three strokes or so, simply scrape them down the curry combs on your thighs, both at the same time. So you are brushing and cleaning like this: left, right, left, right, left, right, scrape, scrape; left, right, left, right, left, right, scrape, scrape! This may sound very funny and you may cause a laugh in the stable the first time you do it (especially if you try to knock the dust out of the curry combs, which really isn't necessary because it will fall out as you move around), but you can cut your body-brush time down by at least half.

Leather-backed brushes mold to fit your hand in time and are easier to hold and therefore more effective in use, than wooden-backed or synthetic ones. They're quite durable, too. About six strokes on one place should be quite enough unless the horse is really dirty. You can also use the two-handed technique with dandy brushes and plastic-toothed curry combs to get off dried mud.

The quickest way to clean out your horse's feet is to walk him through water, but if there is none handy (and you should check for jammed-in stones and loose shoes, anyway) just use your hoof pick in the normal way, ideally from heel to toe so you don't push little stones under the loosest part of the shoe at the heels. Don't forget the sides and cleft of the frog, and automatically check for tenderness there or any foul smell which could indicate thrush developing.

As mentioned earlier in this book, horse vacuums can be a real boon to the tired and harried groomer, especially for very dusty horses and those caked with dried mud. The most effective

> **Grooming is an exercise not of the arm but of the whole body.**

> **A walk through water saves a pick through mud.**

models are the type which combine a rotary brush in the nozzle with the vacuum facility.

Time and energy can also be saved by rinsing off a muddy or sweaty horse with warm, clear water. Soap or shampoo is not necessary unless the horse is very greasy or dirty, and too-frequent shampooing can remove too much natural oil from skin and hair. In suitable weather, a simple hosing or sluicing down with a soft brush (a water-brush being the obvious choice), which is more efficient than a sponge, will clean the horse of sweat, mud and some grease.

Hosing off a sweaty horse in summer is a refreshing way to cool him, but he'll cool more quickly if you use warmish water rather than cold. Horses sweat to lose body heat into the atmosphere through the evaporating moisture. If cold water contacts the warm muscle masses, the surface veins constrict, blocking the blood that needs to unload its heat into the cooler atmosphere, and the horse will take longer to cool off. A warm-water (body temperature) wash, on the other hand,

• encourages the cooling evaporation,

• does not shock the horse as cold water can on a hot body, particularly over the muscle masses of the loins and quarters where the application of cold water can cause cramp,

• cleans the animal better than cold.

If you do want to wash your horse in cold weather, take care to avoid chilling him by doing a bit at a time, drying off in between and keeping the other parts of the horse covered with old blankets while you work.

Mud and Wet

Dealing with mud can be a big problem for working horse owners. If the horse is out in wet, muddy conditions and you are pushed for time when you get to the stables, you will almost certainly not be able to get him dry and tacked up in time to exercise him in your limited time slot. But you needn't worry about getting the outdoor horse bone dry before using him. I have many a time put tack on a wet (not muddy) back and gone out. I have never been able to see the difference between a back wet with sweat under the saddle and one wet with rain. When faced with a muddy back, I have hosed off the mud, gone to work with the sweat scraper, old towels and maybe the hair dryer until the worst of the wet is gone, then saddled up, with saddle pad, and

Does a wet back care if it's sweat or rain?

taken the horse out—and I have never had any problems at all or seen any sign that the horse has been uncomfortable.

An absorbent saddle pad—cotton fleece, quilted cotton or real sheepskin—between horse and saddle makes the horse more comfortable and absorbs moisture. Saddle pads are available in synthetic textiles, which are said to "wick" (draw) moisture away from the horse through the fabric, thereby keeping the horse drier. Regular use of a saddle pad also means you will not need to clean your saddle quite so often. You can use an absorbent girth, too, or pad your leather girth with a fleece cover. Again, "wicking" synthetic textiles are used for girths to help keep the horse drier under them. The girth area is particularly susceptible to friction which leads to rubbing and galling, so anything which helps reduce this problem is worthwhile.

Having a clean horse handy at all times is one of the advantages of using a New Zealand rug or other turnout blanket on outdoor horses. A lightweight waterproof sheet shaped to fit the horse and with properly adjusted leg straps will keep him dry without too much warmth when the weather is mild or the horse is unclipped and will save you a lot of time and effort. Just make sure mud is cleaned off the girth area so you do not encourage rubbing and galls.

Still on the topic of mud, I once received a telling-off from a vet because, having presented him with a case of scratches, I told him all the horse books said to let mud dry under bandages, then brush it off. He told me that we horse owners were all lazy, slovenly and misguided. "You're just asking for trouble," he said. "Rinse it off! You have to get rid of it quickly if your horse is prone to scratches. Dry the legs properly and you'll have no more trouble." He was right; I didn't. He also recommended an emollient barrier cream, such as the zinc-oxide ointment use to guard against diaper rash in infants, as a preventative in susceptible individuals.

It is a moot point whether or not to use water on horses in winter. Some people do it, and, provided the horse is kept warm and dry afterwards, they have no problem. Others never do it but wait until the mud is dry, then brush it off and similarly never have any problems! I belong to the former category, partly because I feel it best to get the horse clean as quickly as possible with the least amount of work. I do prefer lukewarm water, but cold is better than nothing if you are quick. A heat lamp is a big advantage in this situation.

"Thatching" horses is a particularly British approach to getting them dry and cool after work or upon returning wet from turnout. Essentially, what you do is cover his back with straw,

> **Muddy pasterns invite cracked heels.**

which is then covered and held in place by an anti-sweat sheet and/or a spare blanket. The idea of the straw is to keep the horse warm so that the moisture will evaporate fairly quickly; the anti-sweat rug lets it evaporate more effectively and quickly than a closer-woven blanket. If you put the regular blanket directly on the straw inside out, as is often taught, moisture will actually gather through the blanket and make the lining damp. Once the "thatched" horse has dried off and you reblanket him, you are in effect rugging the horse in damp clothing, which is not the best stable management. Using an anti-sweat sheet or an old blanket during thatching eliminates the dampness problem and keeps your stable/night rug dry.

If you use blankets made of fabrics which are said to "breathe" (which means that they allow moisture from the horse to evaporate up through them but prevent rain soaking through) you can, instead of conventionally thatching a horse, simply put an anti-sweat sheet on next to his skin and the rug on top, and the horse will dry off well. This method is especially useful in stables where straw is not used for bedding and is therefore not available for thatching. With "breathable" blankets, the anti-sweat sheet is not essential, but it does seems to help a little with the wetness problem with some rugs.

Blanketing

There is no doubt that a range of good clothing can be of great help in horse management, partly in helping to keep the horse clean and dry and also, of course, in fending off chills. It is much cheaper to keep your horse warm and in good condition by clothing him and sensibly housing and sheltering him than to do so by feeding him large amounts of concentrates. Research with cattle has found that those kept in warm, well-ventilated stables ate up to 25 percent less concentrate than those living outdoors, and although I have no data for horses, it seems reasonable to suppose that similar figures would apply for their food intake.

You need to remember in blanketing horses that they are not nearly so affected by cold temperatures as we are. Studies have shown that horses tolerate dry, still, cold weather down to -4 degrees Fahrenheit (one study said -40 degrees Centigrade) before showing signs of significant stress. However, I have often seen Thoroughbred-type horses on an autumn day, which could be described as no more than chilly but accompanied by wind and rain, who were shivering hard and could not wait to be brought in. Wind and rain exert what is called a "chill factor," which intensifies the cold and can cause considerable suffering

> **Straw stands in cheap for expensive sweat sheets.**

even in hardy breeds. Forcing horses to endure such conditions is cruel and uneconomical as it is almost impossible to feed them enough food to keep weight on; shelter is essential and good clothing highly desirable.

It is up to each owner to decide what is best for his or her own horse, but I believe it is far cheaper and more effective in the long run to buy good-quality clothing and use it when appropriate than to spend extra money on more food in cold weather. Good clothing lasts many years when properly looked after and will recoup its cost in saved feed many times over, particularly when you take into account the effects of inflation and poor harvests which push feed prices sky high.

> **A good turnout rug buys itself with feed not fed.**

If your horse is clipped at all, you are sure to need blankets. If he is doing nothing but light work at weekends in winter, perhaps you could get away with no clip or just a breast clip, where the hair is removed only from the front of the breast and up the gullet. This will be better than no clip at all if he is doing some work, but, particularly with a cold-blooded horse or pony, you may still not have problems with keeping him warm at other times.

With a trace clip, it is often overlooked that the hair has been removed from the underside, the very part of the horse which contacts the mud or cold ground when he lies down. This means his skin has little protection there, so I feel it is quite wrong to consider that a trace-clipped horse with a New Zealand rug will be quite all right out all winter without anywhere dry, such as a bedded shelter, to lie down in out of the weather.

With any horse clothing, good fit is important. Stress to the supplier that you want a rug that is shaped along the spine seam to fit the shape of the horse's back, not cut in a straight line allowing no room for the withers and croup. Rugs should start in front of the withers, not on top of them, and should extend back to the root of the tail. New Zealand rugs should go about six inches past the root of the tail, and some of the best have a drawstring sewn into the back edge of the rug which can be pulled to attain an individual fit.

When the breast straps are fastened, the neckline of the rug should rest round the base of the neck, not come down on to the shoulders. You should be able to pass your hand comfortably round the neckline and should not detect any pull on the points of the shoulders. With New Zealand or other turnout rugs, the horse must be able to get his head down comfortably to graze without pulling the rug on to his withers or half choking himself. At the same time, the breast strap must not be so loose that it allows the rug to slip back unreasonably (although most rugs slip back a little). Modern rugs without round-the-girth surcingles but with various designs of leg straps or with diagonally-crossing underbelly surcingles are far preferable to the old-fashioned kind which, acting like a belt round the horse's middle, inevitably cause some pressure on his spine.

A neck hood may be a helpful addition to a horse's turnout wardrobe as this will certainly keep mud off the neck and mane and so save a lot of cleaning-up time. There are head-and-neck hoods as well although I find that some horses do not like their heads being covered and the head is much less trouble to clean than the neck and mane. The neck hood is usually coordinated with the turnout rug as it needs to fasten to it and overlap the neckline so that water will not seep underneath but with some types of closely-fitting hoods this may not be necessary.

Exercise clothing is also useful in wet weather so you do not have to wait while the horse dries off before rugging him up normally or putting his New Zealand on again to go out into the field. It is not a good plan to put the usual "nonbreathing" New Zealand rug on a horse with a wet coat as the water from the horse will have nowhere to evaporate to and he could stay damp under the rug for a long time and become chilled. The skin is more susceptible to rubbing when wet, too. If you use a New Zealand rug, you should really have two so you can alternate them, keeping them both reasonably clean by regularly brushing or, better yet, vacuuming the linings brushed and oiling the leather fittings.

Blanket upkeep demands a fair amount of your time and energy, but there are laborsaving approaches. Synthetic fabrics save a lot of time in laundering; they dry much more quickly then natural fabrics and are lighter for the horse. At times when he is shedding, a cotton or linen summer sheet next to the horse under his normal clothing helps prevent the latter becoming matted with hairs, which work their way into the fabric and can be impossible to remove entirely. If woollen clothing is used, the sheet can help keep them cleaner so you are not faced with the job of washing thick, heavy clothing so often.

> **A trace-clipped horse turned out in winter's muck is like a down-jacketed man with down-below in swimming trunks.**

Bedding

Apart from giving your horse somewhere comfortable to rest, good bedding in shelter or stable helps keep him warm and so, in its own way, reduces feed costs. It also protects the horse from hair loss, skin abrasions and possible bruising on hard floors.

As mentioned, **deep litter** is unquestionably the most labor- and money-saving method of bedding horse shelters. The longest I have left a deep-litter stall that was bedded in straw was six months over winter, but I know people who have had them down for years without changing them. I have visited them regularly and have never noticed any smell, dampness, foot trouble, vermin or other disadvantages or problems. It is most noticeable that when you walk into the stall or shelter it is just like stepping onto a well-constructed mattress, springy and firm at the same time, and the horses are always quite happy on them. Sawdust, perhaps surprisingly, also makes good deep-litter bedding, but shredded paper is recommended for semi-deep litter only. Shavings scatter more easily than sawdust but are acceptable if the horse is not prone to digging up his bed.

The secret of success in deep litter is to be meticulous about removing droppings. If you miss the odd pile here and there, particularly in an open shed where you may feel it is not quite so important, you will find that your bed soon turns into an indoor muck heap—not at all what you want.

Deep litter is perhaps more suited to winter than summer in most circumstances, and ventilation is always extremely important. With long-established beds, you eventually reach the stage where you are hardly adding any fresh material at all, so the bed seems to stop getting higher yet remains firm, clean and warm. Also, the technique is particularly well-suited to run-in sheds with adequate access for tractors with front-end loaders to do the clean-out honors when the day finally comes.

For those who do not like deep litter of any kind, the time consuming chore of **stall cleaning** has to be done as quickly and thoroughly as possible. The following system offers about the quickest way to get the job done:

- Pick up all obvious droppings first.

- Have a quick stamp or poke around for any piles that are covered up, then, if you dispose of the manure and bedding separately, put all the droppings in their appropriate container/ pile.

- For straw beds, pick out all the clean bedding and pile it in the cleanest corner.

- Then separate all the half-clean bedding into another corner, leaving the thoroughly filthy bedding in the center of the floor.

- Fork this soiled material *en masse* into the largest wheelbarrow or cart you can find (so you don't have to make any more trips to the manure heap than necessary).

- Rake earthen floors and sweep other types of floors with vigor to gather up all the remaining waste, and put it in the barrow.

> **Just a few missed piles do a muck heap make.**

• Dust an earthen floor with hydrated lime or commercial stall "sweetener." For washable floors, occasionally scrub down with hot water and baking soda, which has good deodorizing properties and is less caustic than lime.

• In rebedding the stall, first lay down the semi-clean material, taking care to cover the floor evenly. Next, put down the old clean straw, and finally round out the bed with new material, some of which you may want to bank up round the sides.

Whatever bedding system or material you prefer, the object should always be to keep it as clean and dry as possible. Some say that a damp bed is better for the horse's feet as the moisture helps keep the hoof horn in good condition. It is true that brittle feet are more in need of moisture than oil, but it can't be overlooked that the moisture in bedding is not ordinary water but urine, which has a very bad effect on hooves. Standing a horse in dirty, wet bedding is the quickest way to give him thrush, a fungus infection of the frog which can cause pain and lameness if it progresses far enough. Therefore, I prefer to aim for dryness in my stall floors, and let my horse's feet get their moisture from outside. The horse would not, anyway, want to lie in his own urine if he had a choice, so this is another reason to keep a dry bed.

Keep your horse's mouth wet and his feet dry.

Manure disposal can be a problem in some areas. Of course, if you have the acreage, you can spread it on your own cropland for its fertilizer value. However, it's generally quite unwise to spread stable manure on horse pastures as it may make the grazing unpalatable and will add to the parasite problems where deworming regimes have not been effective.

There may be a market for manure containing straw and also peat moss (although the latter I find a very poor bedding material, being extremely absorbent and always damp and cold in winter and smelly in summer; it is also dusty, contrary to popular opinion). Shavings and sawdust are also not impossible to get rid of. But there is sometimes a problem with shredded paper, which does not seem to have been accepted yet as a manure even though it is biodegradable. Its suppliers often give advice as to how it can be sold, and it is worth contacting the maker of your product on this point. Synthetic bedding materials make their appearance on the market from time to time and can certainly be tried, but it is a good plan to check with the manufacturers first about disposal techniques. Being synthetic, the material will not rot down into a suitable manure, and it is now ecologically unfriendly to burn it (or have garden or refuse fires of any sort, incidentally) and may even result in prosecution in some areas.

Mushroom growers and gardening nurseries often purchase horse manure in straw bedding, and a word with other horse owners or a bit of "finger walking" in your Yellow Pages directory could locate a market. However, commercial growers rarely want to be bothered with picking up the output of one or two backyard horses. If you use the system of stall cleaning which I prefer, that is, making two piles, one comprised almost entirely of droppings and the other of used bedding, you will find the droppings pile relatively easy to get rid of to amateur gardeners and the other useable around your premises. Straw, shavings and sawdust can all be spread thickly on areas, such as gateways, approaches to shelters and around water sources, which become badly pocked in winter. Your horse's play area is also an ideal place to spread it. The material will gradually dry out and rot away, being a natural organic product, so you will not end up with mountains of the stuff around the place. If you deworm your horses properly, there will be no problem with parasite eggs or larvae infecting the land.

The droppings pile can be ready bagged as described, reusing feed and shavings bags to avoid the expense of buying sacks for the purpose. Once local gardeners know your muck really is ninety-percent manure and not bedding, you could well find that you cannot produce enough of it! Commercial buyers, too, will prefer it to the normal bedding-heavy product.

If you take a little care in situating your manure heap, you will find your work greatly lessened. You should try to site it downwind of the house or stables and, probably even more importantly, of your neighbors' homes. It also helps greatly for it to be located in a dip or even a specially constructed pit with a gently sloping ramp so that the considerable job of heaving manure up onto the heap is avoided. Instead, this arrangement allows you to simply tip the wheelbarrow and let gravity take care of the unloading chores.

> **Why struggle and heave, when gravity works without a puff?**

If you have a regular pickup arrangement with a nursery, say, to remove your heap, they may provide a container or trailer into which you put each day's wastes and which they then remove when filled, leaving another in its place. If you are going to use your used bedding on your own premises, it greatly facilitates transport if you dump it straight on to a trailer of your own, then one of the horses can cart it about where needed. There is no reason why Arab or Thoroughbred horses should not help in this way—it does not have to be a job for clodhoppers.

I have already said that caring for a manure pile is a job of the lowest priority in the life of a working owner. If I visit a stable where there is an immaculately groomed, stamped-down, steaming brick of manure in some discreet corner of the stable, I become a little concerned about the welfare of the horses themselves, because I cannot imagine any stable with today's time and labor-saving considerations having the luxury to do such a job and still care properly for the horses.

It is true that compacting the manure pile does make it rot down more effectively and quickly, but most nurseries and particularly mushroom growers want fresh, not rotted, manure. And just left to itself, the heap will rot, if more slowly than with your constant attentions.

Exercise and Fitness

Exercising is certainly the single most time-consuming task in the working owner's schedule, and also one of the most important if the horse is to be kept healthy, let alone fit. I have already stressed the great advantages of having turnout facilities for augmenting under-saddle exercise. In addition to the facilities already discussed, horses in small private stables are often allowed to wander about the place for a bit of "light relief," if only one at a time to prevent shenanigans from arising. However, for developing hard, physical fitness, there is no escaping ridden or driven work, or, to some extent, loose schooling such as jumping, liberty work or, in short doses, lunging or long reining.

The worst months for exercising are obviously those with the fewest daylight hours. December and January are the most difficult times for owners with other daytime commitments, while November and February run a close second. The shortest day of the year is December 21, so after that you can console yourself with the thought that, henceforth, it's all downhill to spring, with milder weather and lighter evenings. A nice thought during the snow and ice of January and February—and maybe of March and April, too!

If you can possibly arrange for some competent person to exercise your horse when you cannot, your life will, of course, be that much easier. Even being ponied from another horse (which again requires a competent horseperson—what an awful word!) is quite useful. If the led horse wears his saddle minus stirrups, this will help keep his skin accustomed to the friction of tack. Tack sores are not uncommon in horses ridden only occasionally as the skin never has chance to harden up.

The amount of exercise a horse gets should depend more on his needs than on his owner's inclinations or time availability, although it is often difficult to reconcile the two. An hour a day, however, is barely enough to keep a horse operating normally, but when combined with turning out, it may be adequate. Working owners who have no access to turnout facilities should, somehow, aim to get their horses exercised for two hours a day if possible. Horses on restricted exercise, especially pony and crossbred types, may hardly need concentrates in their diets, even in winter. Good hay may supply all the energy and other nutrients they require.

Most general exercise is done at the walk, but some steady trotting and canter intervals will have to be included, ground conditions permitting, if fitness is to be maintained. Some people disapprove of trotting on roads but, as described earlier in this book, used wisely it can be an advantage rather than a danger.

If you turn out a concentrate-fed horse in winter, you may well find that his time in the field maintains him at half fitness, particularly if he has the company of other horses to keep him on the move. In this case, much of your planned exercise can be done at this steady trot, lessening the total amount of time you need to spend in the saddle.

Scheduling

In the black mornings of winter, it is very tempting not to tear yourself out of bed in what is still the middle of the night to give your horse his exercise, and if you are only going to work him moderately on weekends it may well not be necessary, provided the horse can be turned out somewhere. But if you want a fairly fit horse, you will have to ride on certainly two and preferably three other days of the week, if only to keep his muscles used to carrying or pulling weight and his skin toughened up enough to withstand the inevitable pressures and friction of even the best-fitting tack or harness.

There is no need to give a horse Sunday off if he has worked on Saturday, provided he has not become unduly tired. Three-day event horses do their hardest work on cross-country/endurance day but still have to show jump on the final day. If your horse works the same way in accordance with his state of fitness, you could give him Monday off, exercise Tuesday, have Wednesday off, exercise Thursday, have Friday off (which will give you a nice fresh horse for Saturday and Sunday). By following this schedule, you can get away with under-saddle exercise on only two work-days/weekdays yet still have a reasonably fit horse.

> **He that riseth late must trot all day**
> **and shall scarce overtake his business at night.**

All this assumes that you do have adequate turnout facilities for the non-riding days. I feel that it is a thoroughly bad practice to leave a horse stabled for even one day without significant exercise (and here I do not count a half-hour of hand walking significant exercise). Think about it from the horse's point of view. Let's say you dismount at 4:00 P.M. on Sunday. You plan to give the horse Monday off, so there's no exercise on Monday morning. By 4:00 A.M. on Monday, he will have had twelve hours without exercise; by 4:00 P.M. on Monday, it will be twenty-four hours; by 4:00 A.M. on Tuesday morning, it will be a mind-boggling thirty-six hours cooped up in a stall without exercise, and if you ride at 7:00 A.M. on Tuesday, the horse will have spent thirty-nine hours (a human's working week) without even enough physical activity to keep the vital juices flowing. If you do not ride until 6:00 P.M. on Tuesday evening, the horse will have been subjected to enforced idleness of body and mind for a horrendous fifty hours! That is more than two whole days. I think even one day without exercise is a terrible thing to do to an animal like a horse who thrives on and needs physical activity for even basic health.

Assuming you can get someone competent to exercise your horse during your workday or even lead him to and from the field, the only possible problem might be insurance. If someone has an accident while supervising your horse, there might be dreadful problems over insurance and compensation one way or another, so discuss your policy very carefully with your broker or a company representative and be quite sure the policy covers all eventualities.

Safety

Most working owners have to do too much of their daily exercising at dusk or even after dark. It is advisable not to do so (certainly never in fog), but many owners have no choice. Floodlit riding rings and indoor arenas are super if you can get to such facilities, but most people cannot. Therefore a few common-sense precautions could save lives of riders forced to go out on public roadways while exercising their horses during times of poor visibility:

• The old-fashioned method of riding facing toward oncoming traffic (in other words, on the left-hand shoulder of the road) so that oncoming traffic can see you (and probably bump right into you) has long been superseded by advice from public-safety experts to travel with the flow of traffic (in other words, on the right-hand shoulder), and this goes for leading in hand, too.

- It may not be unlawful for a horse and rider to go on roads at dusk with no lights, but it is extremely stupid. A horse pulling a carriage or cart must, by law, have lights. Attach a light to the left (traffic-side) stirrup for a ridden horse, one that shows a strong white light to the front and a strong red one to the rear.

- Wear white or pale-colored clothing. The most visible color at night is reflective white; during daylight, orange, yellow or pink are most easily seen.

- Use reflective strips on your horse's leg wraps or boots rather than on some relatively stationery piece of equipment, such as his exercise sheet. Studies have shown that motorists slow down significantly when they pick up moving reflective items as this seems to confuse them more than relatively static reflecting equipment.

- Look in tack shops and sports stores catering to joggers and cyclists for reflective crossbelts, hat covers, arm/wrist bands and the like with which to outfit yourself. Better yet, try to locate safety gear with battery-powered lights as opposed to just reflectors or reflective strips. Lights are by far more effective in making you and your horse more visible after dark.

One thing is sure: you are not safe on the public roadways, no matter how dependable your horse may be or how impeccably you follow the rules of the road, if you cannot be seen.

Footing

Exercising can prove difficult in winter if the roads become icy and bridle paths and other areas become too waterlogged, muddy or rutted to use. Years ago, it was fairly common for horses and ponies who had to work daily to earn their owners' livings to be shod with frost nails. These are not studs but actual horseshoe nails with little "pimples" of hardened metal on the ground surface of the nail. Such nails are still used to shoe horses who race on frozen lakes in Switzerland and Canada and similar countries, so it could be worthwhile discussing the matter of nonslip footwear with your farrier to see if it might facilitate exercising for you in icy conditions.

If all else fails, you will have to turn to that pile of used bedding to lay a track round your stable or somewhere else suitable, and ride the horses on that. However, if a play area is provided or you have some kind of outdoor schooling area, you will probably find that these are the last to freeze, and your used bedding spread on top anyway will make them quite useable in hard weather.

> **Visibility is the better part of safety.**

Seasonal Adaptations

From winter, to summer. Here the main problem with turning horses out for exercise is the flies. Some of the popular repellents work for only a short time and some appear not to work at all. One type of product that works better than most other is what is termed a "residual" repellent. Agricultural suppliers have stocked them for many years due to the damage caused to cattle hides by warble flies; these repellents remain active for two or three days (not hours) but if conditions are suitable—no rain and the horse not being made to sweat much—they can work for up to ten days. Of course, you'll have to keep a watchful eye to see that they are still effective and apply more if they are not. It is best to start using them in spring before flies arrive so that a good level of protection will have built up in the coat by summertime. If you habitually wash your horse, you will have to be sure to reapply the product after each wash.

> **Be there a repellent so sure, that flies don't alight for ten minutes . . . or more?**

Most repellents come in spray-on containers, and it is a common objection among owners that they cannot use them because their horses are afraid of the spray. The product can always be sprayed on to a rag, of course, and wiped on that way, but why not simply train your horse to get used to it? If you can train him to get used to traffic, jumping fences and being clipped and shod, then surely he can get used to a spray. Try stuffing cotton in his ears and playing the radio or even singing so he cannot hear the noise of the spray. Do not spray his head, of course, but apply the repellent with a rag on ears, forelock and face. It is often the horse's eyes which receive much of the flies' attention, as they feed on the discharges. Their irritations produce more discharge which, in turn, attracts more flies, and so it goes on. Check the label for cautions about using the product on sensitive areas, such as around eyes and on sheath and dock areas, and, if the product appears to be safe, apply it there where protection is really needed.

You may ultimately prefer to stable your horse during the day and turn him out at night. However, there are such things as night-flying insects, as well, so a repellent is still a valuable aid to your horse's comfort and well-being and should enable you to turn him out for exercise without exposing him to insect attacks.

If the ground becomes baked hard in summer and your horse is not shod, you may experience problems with chipped and broken feet, and, as a result, a footsore horse. So it may be necessary to have the horse shod, even if he is resting, perhaps just with a lightweight shoe. Exercising without shoes is quite feasible provided ground conditions are relatively soft or smooth and the hooves are regularly trimmed to maintain correct balance. Smooth, hard roads are no problem but gritted, chipped or stony surfaces should be avoided. The horse needs a good diet to produce sound hoof wall and a good foot conformation, with no flat soles and shelly horn to get through fly-stomping and summer-hacking season without shoes.

A fit, regularly worked horse causes his owner less work than does a soft, unfit one who requires a strict, regularly carried-out fitness program to gradually bring him into better shape. Grooming is also comparatively effortless on fit horses—they seem to keep much cleaner than idle ones. Exercise is so very important to horses that every effort should be made to provide it by any means at our disposal.

> **Cleanliness is next to fitness, while idleness and fat snuggle up to filth.**

It is hoped that the methods detailed and ideas put forward in this book will be taken in the spirit in which they were intended, that is, to help busy horse owners look after their horses not only properly but perhaps, from the horses' points of view, even better than might otherwise have been the case because of the emphasis on extra freedom and liberty stressed throughout. The corners I have advised cutting will not result in any deterioration in the standard of horse care, and may well be adopted by those with more time than the average working owner in order to free up time for other things.

I have sometimes advised spending money to save time, and there's no escaping the fact that it's indeed sometimes necessary to spend one in order to save the other. The working horse owner's scarcest commodity is usually time, although money is a close second, and the equipment I have suggested really can help get things done so much more quickly that it is usually regarded as a sound investment.

> **Beware of little expenses; a small leak will sink a great ship.**

The main thing is to get your priorities right, placing the most importance on those jobs which directly affect your horse. He will then be properly and well looked after, and you should find that you can care for him in less time than you ever thought possible—and in the long run, I hope, more cheaply—to the benefit of both of you.

Recipes for Success

Precisely how individual horse owners manage to get their horses cared for on a day-to-day, hour-to-hour basis can be decided only by their individual circumstances. The following schedules are ones which I personally have used and which worked well for me. They may serve as guides to owners trying to formulate daily programs to insure adequate care of horses or ponies kept under varying conditions at different times of year.

The Stabled Horse

Stabled animals are not so much at the mercy of the weather as those kept at pasture or on the combined system (partly in and partly out). The following routine, therefore, is basically applicable at any time of year for an owner with an ordinary nine-to-five job. The references to winter tasks, such as fitting reflective clothing or attending to blankets, can simply be ignored in summer.

Early morning

Check horse for signs of normality or otherwise. Check droppings for consistency, odor, color and number. Check stall for signs of restlessness, such as churned-up bedding and scrabble marks on walls that could indicate the horse was cast during the night or had a colic attack. Check hay eaten/feed finished/water drunk. All this should take you about one minute.

Pick up droppings or clean stall completely and leave floor bare, depending on bedding system used. Give the saddle and bridle areas a quick brushing and pick out feet. Tack up/ harness and put to, including safety light and reflective clothing if appropriate. Exercise. If raining and cold, trot home to keep horse warm.

On return, put away tack and hang exercise clothing (if worn) to dry. If horse is wet in winter, leave standing under infrared lamp with a full haynet in reach. Bed down the stall or add new material to deep or semi-deep litter. Give two buckets of water or check that automatic waterer is working and clean. Blanket horse, using an anti-sweat sheet under rug, if he is still damp. Return him to stall; give breakfast.

Leave midday feed/hay ready for helper to give, if possible.

Finally, check breakfast eaten, top off water, pick up droppings if necessary. Leave for work.

Midday (if help available)

Check and adjust blankets, removing anti-sweat sheet, if appropriate. Pick up droppings. Feed. Top off hay/water.

Evening

Check, groom and tack up horse quickly, same as early morning. Use lights and reflective clothing, as needed, and exercise/lunge/lead in hand to graze. After exercise, put away tack, etc. and stand horse under infrared lamp if wet. Pick out feet/check shoes. Give water and full haynet(s). Pick up droppings and replenish/fluff up bedding. Groom horse if dry. Blanket; return to stall; feed.

Late evening (if at all possible)

Check horse, as usual. Remove anti-sweat sheet; groom if not done before; rug up normally for night, or readjust rugs. Leave full haynet(s) and two buckets of water. Pick up droppings/ fluff up bedding. Feed, if required.

Leave dry feeds ready mixed for morning, fill haynet(s). Take exercise clothing home to dry.

The Pasture-Kept Horse

Winter

A pasture-kept horse in winter needs only a little less attention than a stabled one. If he is expected to, say, hunt or do other strenuous work on Saturdays, he will still need ridden or driven work on two or three days a week to keep him fit enough. The exercise he gives himself in the field will keep him "ticking over" but will not maintain hard fitness. A suggested daily routine for a pasture-kept horse in winter, on a day when he is being ridden/driven, is as follows:

Early morning Catch horse and tie up in shelter or spare stall. Remove turnout rug. Check horse for well-being, especially for signs of exposure ailments, such as scratches and rain rot, runny eyes, chapped face and loss of condition, and run your hands through unclipped areas of his coat, feeling for injuries or skin ailments. Pick out feet and tidy up as best you can. Tack up/harness and put to, adding lights and reflective clothing if needed. A light, waterproof sheet will be needed during exercise if raining, as turnout rugs cannot be replaced on wet horse without risking chill/skin problems, and you won't have time to wait for horse to dry before going to work.

On returning from exercise, feed (separately from other horses if necessary), top off hay in shelter, check water supply. Pick up droppings shelter. Replace/change turnout rug. Padlock field gate both ends. Put away tack/harness; hang exercise sheet somewhere to dry.

Evening Check and groom horse as morning, paying special attention to feet and legs and underside of horse for signs of scratches and his back and neck for rain rot. Take horse into stable, if possible; wash off mud, rinse and dry pasterns and heels thoroughly and apply preventative cream before returning horse to field. (This sounds overprotective, but if horse is susceptible to scratches this is much less trouble, in the long run, than having to deal with actual ailment, which can be very stubborn and require stabling and veterinary treatment.)

Horse can be eating feed while you do above. Also, go over him with a brush, check feet/shoes, put on turnout blanket and return to field. Top off hay, check water, pick up droppings in the shelter and replenish bedding. Padlock gate both ends.

(If your pasture shelter has no electricity, a battery-operated lantern, which can be hung up somewhere while you work, is convenient for your after-dark labors.)

If the horse is a very hardy type, wintering out without a New Zealand rug and maybe without a shelter either, extra vigilance will be needed on the owner's part. The horse cannot be clipped if living in such conditions, and there may be times when he's too wet to wear tack or harness; either skip the weekday exercise or use saddle pads of fabric that wicks moisture away from the skin. A very watchful eye must be kept for ailments and loss of condition; the horse should be regularly groomed and examined and his feet and shoes picked out/checked daily.

Summer

Early morning Check horse; groom tack-contact areas; pick out feet. Tack up/harness and put to. Exercise. On return, feed if appropriate, pick up droppings in shelter, check water supply, put hay in shelter, if paddock bare. Padlock gate both ends. Put away tack/harness, etc. Leave for work.

Evening Check horse; groom tack-contact areas; pick out feet. If working, tack up/harness and put to. Exercise. On return, feed if appropriate, pick up droppings in shelter, check water, put hay in shelter, if necessary. Padlock gate both ends. Put away tack/harness, etc. and leave.

Combined-System Horse

This is an ideal system for the working horse owner, winter or summer, and is certainly the one to aim for if at all possible.

Winter

The following routine is suggested for a horse who is trace or chaser clipped and whose owner works all day.

Early morning Check horse, groom and pick out feet exactly as for stabled horse. If exercising, tack up/harness and put to, using safety lights/reflective clothing if appropriate. Exercise, using waterproof exercise sheet, if raining. On return, stand horse under infrared lights to dry, put away tack/harness. Put exercise clothing to dry. Feed horse and put on appropriate turnout rug. While he's eating, put day's hay supply in shelter, check water supply and prepare midday feed for helper to give, if possible. Turn horse out. Clean stall, leaving floor bare, or pick up droppings if deep litter. Leave for work.

Evening   Bed stall/replenish bedding, hang up full haynet(s) and give two buckets of water or check waterer. Bring horse in, remove blanket and check carefully for injuries sustained in field. Groom; wash/cream legs as for pasture-kept horse if susceptible to scratches. Otherwise, rinse off mud, dry thoroughly and bandage legs. Put on stable blanket; take turnout blanket home to dry.

Late evening (if possible)   Check horse. Adjust rugs. Top off hay/water. Pick up droppings/ fluff up bedding. Feed, if required. Leave grain ration ready for morning.

Summer

Early morning   Bed stall/replenish bedding. Bring horse in and check. Groom/pick out feet and check shoes. If exercising, tack up/harness and put to. Exercise. On return, put away tack/ harness. Give full haynet(s), water and feed. Leave horse in for day, away from flies.

Midday (if help available)   Check horse. Pick up droppings in stall. Feed/hay/water.

Evening   Check horse; feed if appropriate; turn out for night. Clean stall, leaving floor bare overnight, or pick up droppings if on deep litter (not normally recommended for summer unless stall very well ventilated). Pick up droppings in shelter, replenish bedding, if appropriate. Check water supply. Put hay in shelter, if paddock bare. Padlock gate both ends.

It is stressed that these routines are only suggestions of successful ways of getting everything done that needs to be done on a daily basis. Tack/harness can be cleaned as/when there is time—at home in the evening rather than wasting "stable" time. Other jobs can be fitted in, probably during weekends, or on days when no exercising is taking place in the case of the pasture-kept or combined-system horse. Owners may prefer to schedule exercise for the evenings rather than for mornings for horses who enjoy regular turnout and therefore need exercising only once a day. These routines are flexible enough to be altered to suit such individual preferences. The important point is that all essential jobs are listed and, by following these routines and fitting them in with your own daily timetable, you can be sure you are doing everything necessary to care for your horse adequately.

Do you *Really* Need to Call the Vet

Veterinarians cost money, but their services are essential not only in curing sickness and in treating injuries but in helping, by means of preventive medicine, to keep our horses healthy. Most horse owners are, at some time or other, presented with a situation where they do not know whether they really need to call the vet or not. If they delay, the horse could become worse and treatment more prolonged and expensive, or the delay could even kill the horse. If they call the vet and the situation turns out to be nothing serious or "fixes" itself before the vet arrives, they have wasted a not inconsiderable call fee and the vet's time, which could have been more usefully spent on a more urgent matter.

The following flow charts are designed to help you decide whether or not to bring in the vet now or wait and see how things develop. *It cannot be stressed too much, however, that if you are in doubt, it is far better to make an appointment for the vet to see the horse or at least telephone him or her for advice than to risk aggravating a potentially serious condition through delay.*

Some signs apply to many different disorders, and though diagnosis is the vet's job, horses' regular caretakers are in the best position to know, or simply sense, that an animal is not quite "right" and should at least be watched. These charts cannot cover every eventuality, but they cover the main signs that should alert your attention. It is hoped that they will provide a quick and easy aid to making the right decision.

Flow chart 1: Bleeding

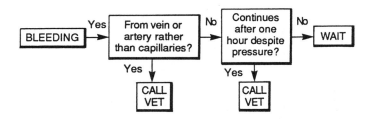

Flow chart 2: Respiration

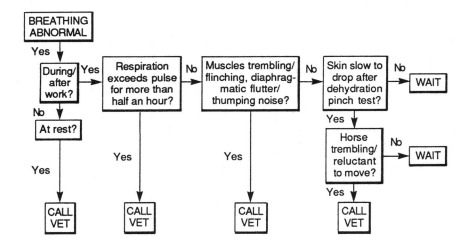

Flow chart 3: Coughing

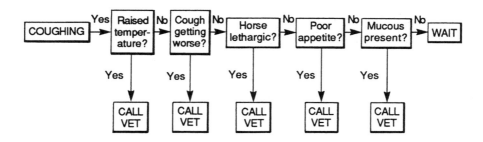

Flow chart 4: Digestive and gastric abnormalities

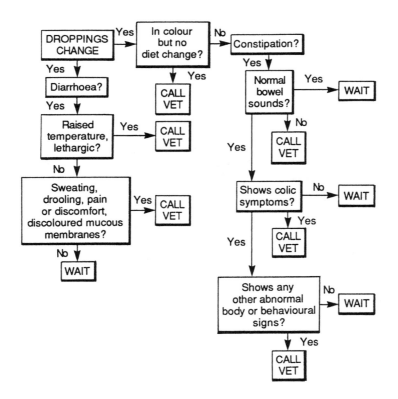

Flow chart 5: Abnormal gait

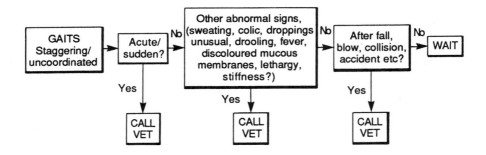

Flow chart 6: Lameness

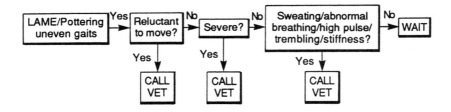

Flow chart 7: Salivation or choking

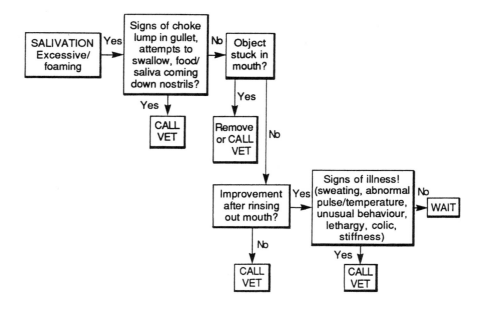

Flow chart 8: Swelling

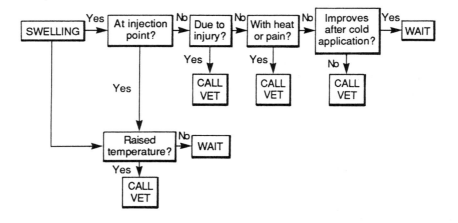

Flow chart 9: Abnormal temperature

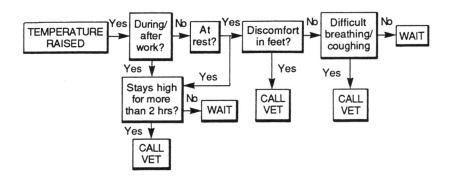

Flow chart 10: Urinary symptoms

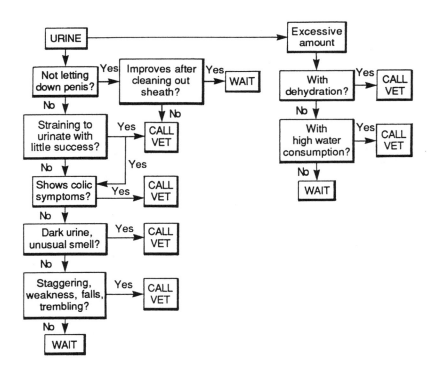

Calculating Your Horse's Weight

Ponies

Girth in inches	40	42.5	45	47.5	50	52.5	55	57.5
Girth in cm	101	108	114	120	127	133	140	146
Bodyweight in lb	100	172	235	296	368	430	502	562
Bodyweight in kg	45	77	104	132	164	192	234	252

Horses

Girth in inches	55	57.5	60	62.5	65	67.5
Girth in cm	140	146	152	159	165	171
Bodyweight in lb	538	613	688	776	851	926
Bodyweight in kg	240	274	307	346	380	414

Girth in inches	70	72.5	75	77.5	80	82.5
Girth in cm	178	184	190	199	203	206
Bodyweight in lb	1014	1090	1165	1278	1328	1369
Bodyweight in kg	453	486	520	570	593	611

Tables based on work of Glushanok, Rochlitz and Skay, 1981

Sources for Tack
and Other
Horse-Care Products

The joys and chores of keeping a horse are made more rewarding when you have at hand the right tools and equipment for the job. If you have trouble locating them, the following list may be of help. It provides the names and headquarter locations for major manufacturers and distributors of the types of horse-care equipment mentioned in this book (no brand names are given). Keep in mind that many companies have products in other categories besides those under which they are listed.

FEED SUPPLIES/EQUIPMENT

Feed/stall charts

Lettersigns Inc.
Tucker, GA

Noble Beast Graphics
Cedar Ridge, CA

Scott Sign Systems Inc.
Tellevast, FL

Feed scoops

Aero Horse Products
Huntington Beach, CA

Dan's Saddlery
Div. Chem-Tainers Ind.
N. Babylon, NY

Fortex/Fortiflex Inc.
San Juan, PR

K&D Plastics Inc.
Gainesville, TX

Horsemen's Pride Inc.
Ravenna, OH

Maidware Products Inc.
Newark, OH

Miller Mfg. Co.
South St. Paul, MN

Rubbermaid Agricultural
Products Inc.
Winchester, VA

Southwest Agriplastics Inc.
Carrollton, TX

Feed, concentrate or supplement

Acco Feed
Minneapolis, MN

Agland of the Rockies
Eaton, CO

Cargill
Nutrena Feed Div.
Minneapolis, MN

Farnam Companies Inc.
Omaha, NE

Life Data Labs Inc.
Cherokee, AL

Milk Specialties Co.
Dundee, IL

Pennwoods Equine Prods. Inc.
Centre Hall, PA

Purina Mills Inc.
St. Louis, MO

Stamina Plus
Cody, WY

Vita-Flex Nutrition Co.
Staten Island, NY

Feed, conditioner

Agri-Products Inc.
Cleveland, OH

Farnam Companies Inc.
Omaha, NE

Ewing, John, Co.
LaSalle, CO

Gateway Products
Holly, CO

Supersweet Feeds
Minneapolis, MN

TEQ Products
Elmont, NY

Feed supplements, vitamin and mineral

Berlin Industries Inc.
Berlin Center, OH

Franklin Laboratories
Div. American Home Prods.
Fort Dodge, IA

Ft. Dodge Laboratories
Fort Dodge, IA

Source Inc.
N. Branford, CT

Superior Feeds Inc.
New Church, VA

U.S. Animal Nutrition
Essex Junction, VT

Vita-Flex
Staten Island, NY

Grain feeders, corner

Dan's Saddlery
N. Babylon, NY

Farnam Companies Inc.
Omaha, NE

Fortex/Fortiflex
San Juan, PR

Horsemen's Pride Inc.
Ravenna, OH

K&D Plastics Inc.
Gainesville, TX

Maidware Products Inc.
Newark, OH

Miller Mfg. Co. Inc.
South St. Paul, MN

Rubbermaid Agricultural
Products Inc.
Winchester, VA

Southwest Agri-Plastics Inc.
Carrollton, TX

Grain feeders, trough

Farnam Companies Inc.
Omaha, NE

Newport Blacksmith Shop
Gordonville, PA

Haynets, bags

Armstrong Supply Co.
Div. of Alexander Ind.
Chattanooga, TN

Holcomb Products Inc.
Madera, CA

Waterbury Rope Mills
Deerfield Beach, FL

Western Heritage Tack Co.
Wichita, KS

Hayracks

Alliance Products
McKinney, TX

Carsbe Co. Inc.
Chattanooga, TN

Centaur Fabricating Corp.
Mira Loma, CA

Happy Horse Products
East Northport, NY

Newport Blacksmith Shop
Gordonville, PA

Partrade Inc.
Denver, CO

Port-A-Stall Corp.
Mesa, AZ

FENCING SUPPLIES

Post and rail fencing

Franklin Equipment Co.
Monticello, IA

Rudl Fence Mfg. Inc.
Weldon, NC

TimberClad Technologies
Jacksonville, TX

Electric fencing

Hot Caps Inc.
Parker, CO

Parker McCrory Mfg. Co.
Kansas City, MO

Woven wire fencing

Keystone Steel and Wire Co.
Peoria, IL

MidStates Wire
Div. MCM Enterprises
Crawfordsville, IN

Synthetic fencing

Alcan Pipe/Kroy Industries
York, NE

Centaur HTP Fencing
Muscle Shoals, AL

Color Guard Fence Co.
Sheboygan, WI

Humane Mfg. Co.
Baraboo, WI

Jump PVC Inc.
Jackson, MO

Lally Tubular Co.
Orland Park, IL

Max-Flex Fence Systems
West Virginia Fence Corp.
Lindside, WV

Mico Fence Systems Inc.
Findlay, OH

Nebraska Plastics Inc.
Cozad, NE

Tensar Polytechnologies Inc.
Morrow, GA

FLY CONTROL

Fly hoods

Double E Fly Way
Sacramento, CA

Farnam Companies Inc.
Omaha, NE

Young, W.F., Inc.
Springfield, MA

Fly repellents

Bickmore Inc.
Hudson, MA

Dionne Products,Div. Qualis Inc.
Des Moines, IA

Farnam Companies Inc.
Omaha, NE

J.M. Saddler Inc.
San Antonio, TX

Starbar, Div. of Zoecon Corp.,
Sandoz Ltd.
Dallas, TX

Tomlyn Products
Buena, NJ

Young, W.F., Inc.
Springfield, MA

Fly control

Arbico
Tucson, AZ

Farnam Companies Inc.
Omaha, NE

Hess & Clark Inc.
Ashland, OH

Spalding Laboratories
Arroyo Grande, CA

GROOMING SUPPLIES

Brushes

Black Forest Saddlery
Crestwood, KY

Brush-Ette Inc.
Menlo Park, CA

Kong Co.
Lakewood, CO

Protecto Horse Equipment Inc.
Clawson, MI

White Horse Trading
Ashland, OR

Wright-Bernet Inc.
Hamilton, OH

Curry combs

Citation Saddlery
Div. Industrial Liaison Inc.
Costa Mesa, CA

Decker Mfg. Co.
Keokuk, IA

Protecto Horse Equipment Inc.
Clawson, MI

Grooming caddies/organizers

Nordic National
Eden Prairie, MN

Pioneer Western Mfg.
Garden Grove, CA

Warner's Tack Mfg. Corp.
Baldwin Park, CA

Hair clippers

Andis Co.
Racine, WI

Double K Industries Inc.
Northridge, CA

Laube Products Sales
Van Nuys, CA

Oster Professional Products
McMinnville, TN

Wahl Clipper Corp.
Sterling, IL

Shampoo

Alto Labs Inc.
Eagan, MN

Exhibitor Labs
Newbury Park, CA

Farnam Companies Inc.
Omaha, NE

Hawthorne Products Inc.
Dunkirk, IN

Healthy HairCare Products
LBI Inc.
Sellersville, PA

NCN Inc.
Bedford, TX

Rio Vista
Santa Barbara, CA

Shapley, Henry E. Ltd.
Waterloo, IA

Straight Arrow Health
Products Inc.
Bethlehem, PA

Farnam Companies Inc.
Omaha, NE

Tomlyn Products
Buena, NJ

Sweat scrapers

Hanco Inc.
Portland, OR

Morgan's
Ellsworth, NE

North & Judd
Middletown, CT

Partrade Inc.
Denver, CO

Super Swipe
Berrien Springs, MI

Vacuum cleaners

Electric Cleaner Co. Inc.
Osseo, WI

Equivac Mfg. Corp.
Bryan, TX

Metropolitan Vacuum Cleaner Co.
Suffern, NY

Parker McCrory Mfg.
Kansas City, MO

Royal Appliance Mfg. Co.
Cleveland, OH

Tack Room, The
Waterloo, IA

Wind River Inc., Wilton Div.
Boise, ID

HOOF CARE PRODUCTS AND EQUIPMENT

Hoof conditioners

Bickmore Inc.
Hudson, MA

Centaur Equine Products
Toledo, OH

Farnam Companies Inc.
Omaha, NE

Life Data Labs Inc.
Cherokee, AL

Racehorse Veterinary Products
Paris, KY

Straight Arrow Health
Products Inc.
Bethlehem, PA

Vapco Inc.
Boston, MA

Young, W.F., Inc.
Springfield, MA

Hoof care tools

Anvil Brand Shoe Co. Inc.
Lexington, IL

Black Forest Saddlery
Crestwood, KY

Buzzard's Roost Equine Supply Inc.
Cave City, KY

Centaur Forge Ltd.
Burlington, WI

Citation Saddlery
Costa Mesa, CA

Multi Products Co.
Lockeford, CA

Nordic Forge Inc.
Guttenberg, IA

North & Judd
Middletown, CT

St. Croix Forge Inc.
Forest Lake, MN

HORSE CLOTHING

Blankets, coolers, sheets

Big D Products
Fairfield, CA

Classic Cover-Ups
West Grove, PA

Curvon Horse Blankets
Tinton Falls, NJ

Equitogs
Devore, CA

Jack's Mfg. Inc.
Washington C.H., OH

Peakes, Ronie & Son
Oxford, MA

Saratoga Horseworks, The
Amsterdam, NY

Triple Crown Blanket
Div. Frehejan Farms Ltd.

W'underwear
Chester Springs, PA

Hoods

Curvon Horse Blankets
Tinton Falls, NJ

Jack's Mfg. Inc.
Washington C.H., OH

Peakes, Ronie & Son
Oxford, MA

Saratoga Horseworks, The
Amsterdam, NY

W'underwear
Chester Springs, PA

Supersweats
Norco, CA

New Zealand Rugs

New Zealand Down Under
Tack Co.

HORSE HEALTH CARE PRODUCTS

Boticides

Farnam Companies Inc.
Omaha, NE

Young, W.F., Inc.
Springfield, MA

Ointments

Corona Products
Div. Summit Industries Inc.
Marrietta, GA

Farnam Companies Inc.
Omaha, NE

Horse Health Products Inc.
Mundelein, IL

Straight Arrow Health Products Inc.
Bethlehem, PA

Uckele Animal Health Corp.
Blissfield, MI

Young, W.F., Inc.
Springfield, MA

Wormers

Beecham Laboratories
Div. Beecham Inc.
Bristol, TN

Davis & Lawrence
Horse Care Products
Cambridge, ONTARIO

Farnam Companies Inc.
Omaha, NE

Ft. Dodge Laboratories
Ft. Dodge, IA

Miles Inc.
Animal Health Div.

Pfizer Inc., Ag. Div.
New York, NY

Wound dressings

Cut-Heal Animal Care Products Inc.
Cedar Hill, TX

Farnam Companies Inc.
Omaha, NE

Horse Health Products Inc.
Mundelein, IL

Horseman's Dream
Div. SportsCare Intl.
Fort Worth, TX

Racehorse Veterinary Products
Paris, KY

SmithKlineBeechamAnimal Health
Exton, PA

Tomlyn Products
Buena, NJ

HORSE IDENTIFICATION

Horse record keeping products

Fauna Forms
Cincinnati, OH

Forus Enterprises
Guntersville, AL

Hi Pack Software
Littleton, CO

Lifetime Companion Animal
Records Co.
Golden, CO

Port-A-Stall
Mesa, AZ

Printed Horse, The
Fort Collins, CO

HORSE TOYS

Horseballs Ltd.
Rockville, MD

Nordic National
Eden Prairie, MN

Smith Brothers Roping Supplies
Denton, TX

HORSE TRAILERS/VANS

Brenderup Trailers
Midland, TX

Featherlite Mfg. Inc,
Grand Meadow, MN

Merhow Industries
Bristol, IN

Sooner Trailer Mfg. Co. Inc.
Duncan, OK

Sundowner
Coleman, OK

Trail-et Inc.
Waupaca, WI

Turnbow Trailers Inc.
Oilton, OK

HORSE INSURANCE

Horse Insurance Specialists Inc.
Pilot Point, TX

Newton Baker Insurance
Services Inc.
Lakeview, NC

North American Horsemen's Assn.
Div. Ark International Group
Paynesville, MN

Rhulen Agency
Monticello, NY

Ziplow Horse Insurance
Baltimore, MD

MECHANICAL WALKERS

Globe Horse Walker
Belton, TX

Hot to Trot Products
Chardon, OH

Imperial Sterling Horsewalker Co.
Naples, FL
Lucas Horse Walker

Supreme Horse Walker Co.
Florence, AL

REFLECTIVE CLOTHING

Horsin' Around Inc.
West Chester, PA

Sun Graphics
Pottstown, PA

REFLECTIVE TACK

Circle Z Trading
Sunnyside, WA
Feathertouch Niterider Safety
Products

Ronmar Industries Inc.
Roswell, GA

Tail Lights Mfg.
Placentia, CA

STABLE EQUIPMENT AND SUPPLIES

Blanket racks

Centaur Fabricating Corp.
Mira Loma, CA

Dudley Equine Equipment
Hugo, OK

Newport Blacksmith Shop
Gordonville, PA

Northrun Saddlery Inc.
Ashland, VA

Partrade Inc.
Denver, CO

Warner's Tack Mfg. Corp.
Baldwin Park, CA

Bridle and halter racks

Champion Horse Supply Co.
Yaphank, NY

Custom Stable Equipment
Pittstown, NJ

Equestrian Forge
Leesburg, VA

Mast Harness Shop
Arthur, IL

Port-A-Stall Corp.
Mesa, AZ

Tac Rex Co.
Appleton, WI

Top Notch Rack
San Dimas, CA

Warner's Tack Mfg. Corp.
Baldwin Park, CA

Wembly Riding Equipment
Alpharetta, GA

Gates

Dudley Equine Equipment
Hugo, OK

Farnam Companies Inc.
Omaha, NE

Gold Bar Livestock Equipment Inc.
Matthews, IN

Northrun Saddlery Inc.
Ashland, VA

Port-A-Stall Corp.
Mesa, AZ

Priefert Mfg. Co.
Mt. Pleasant, TX

Rohn Agri Products
Peoria, IL

VaFac Inc.
Fredericksburg, VA

Muck buckets

Dan's Saddlery
New Babylon, NY

Fortex/Fortiflex
San Juan, PR

Horsemen's Pride Inc.
Ravenna, OH

K&D Plastics Inc.
Gainesville, TX

Maidware Products Inc.
Newark, OH

Miller Mfg. Co.
South St. Paul, MN

Rubbermaid Agricultural
Products Inc.
Winchester, VA

Southwest Agri-Plastics Inc
Carrollton, TX

Saddle racks

American Aluminum Accessories
Perry, FL

Armstrong Supply Co.
Div. Alexander Industries
Chattanooga, TN

Custom Creations
Oneida, TN

D & M Tack
Prior Lake, MN

Hang-Tite Inc.
Bend, OR

Port-A-Stall Corp.
Mesa, AZ

Saddle-Lite
Wilmette, IL

Tack Barn, The
Winder, GA

Top Notch Rack
San Dimas, CA

Warner's Tack Mfg. Corp.
Baldwin Park, CA

Stable bedding

Hillsboro Wood Products Inc.
Hillsboro, OH

Rice Hull Specialty Products
Stuttgart, AR

Running Bear Farm Inc.
Kitts Hills, OH

Stable brooms

Empire Brushes Inc.
Greenville, NC

Union Tools
Columbus, OH

Wright-Bernet
Hamilton, OH

Stable forks

Apple Picker Inc.
Mesa, AZ

K&D Plastics Inc.
Gainesville, TX

Miller Mfg. Co.
South St. Paul, MN

Union Tools
Columbus, OH

Stalls

B-J Mfg. Inc.
Harrison, AR

Barncrafter
Phoenix, AZ

Port-A-Stall Corp.
Mesa, AZ

Stall mats

Ace Rubber Products
Akron, OH

Equustall/A.C.F. Inc
Richmond, VA

Humane Mfg. Co.
Baraboo, WI

Sterling Enterprises
Rocky Face, GA

White Horse Trading Co.
Louisville, KY

Stall sweeteners

ACR Ltd.
Stratford, CT

Greentree Laboratories Inc.
Tustin, CA

Recovery Equine Products
Boxford, MA

Steelhead Specialty Minerals
Spokane, WA

Zirin Laboratories Int. Inc.
Pembroke Pines, FL

Tack trunks

Dan's Saddlery
New Babylon, NY

Tackwood Co.
Taneytown, MD

Tobruk Equine Service
Dandridge, TN

Warner's Tack Mfg. Corp.
Baldwin Park, CA

Wheelbarrows/carts

Dan's Saddlery
Div. Chem-Tainer Ind.
New Babylon, NY

KADCO Inc.
Saratoga Springs, NY

Rubbermaid Agricultural
Products Inc.
Winchester, VA

TACK AND SADDLERY

Girths/cinches

Bar S Cincha and Supply
Canyon, TX

Carsbe Co. Inc.
Chattanooga, TN

Fabri-Tech Inc.
Fishers, IN

Fits-Em Mfg.
Indianapolis, IN

Hergon Saddle-Cinch Factory Inc.
Denver, CO

Just Merino Sheepskin Products
McNeal, AZ

Montana Cincha
Absarokee, MT

Moreland, Dennis Enterprises
Eagle Pass, TX

Ulster International Inc.
New Paltz, NY

Western Cinch Co.
Moab, UT

Western Heritage Tack Co. Inc.
Wichita, KS

Halters, leather

Ballard's Leather
Bloomington, CA

Blue Ribbon Leather
Shelbyville, TN

Champion Turf Equipment Inc.
Los Angeles, CA

Congress Leather Co.
Kingville, OH

Courbette Saddlery Co. Inc.
Heath, OH

Crate's Leather Co.
Chattanooga, TN

Herrmann, H.D., Inc.
Vallejo, CA

Schneider Saddlery
Billy Royal Div.
Bainbridge, OH

Tex Tan Western Leather
Yoakum, TX

Weaver Leather Co.
Mt. Hope, OH

Halters, nylon

Fabtron Inc. (Flip-Whip)
Maryville, TN

Hamilton Halter Mfg. Co.
Ocala, FL

Parker Enterprises
Harrison, AR

Ronmar Industries Inc.
Roswell, GA

Stockmen's Inc.
Lawton, IA

T.R. Tack Supply
Jenks, OK

Valhoma Industries Inc.
Tulsa, OK

Weaver Leather Inc.
Mount Hope, OH

Saddle pads, absorbent

Canterbury Inc.
Quakertown, PA

Classic Sheepskins
Temecula, CA

Diamond Wool Products
Cumberland, RI

French Creek Tack
French Creek, WV

Ulster International Inc.
New Paltz, NY

Saddles, adustable trees

Australian Stock Saddle Co.
Malibu, CA

JT International Dist. Inc.
Indianapolis, IN

Performance Saddlery Inc.
Ithaca, NY

Saddles, synthetic

American Saddlery Inc.
Chattanooga, TN

JT International Dist. Inc.
Indianapolis, IN

Big Horn Inc.
Chattanooga, TN

Miller's Harness Co.
E. Rutherford, NJ

Ulster International Inc.
New Paltz, NY

WATERING SUPPLIES AND EQUIPMENT

Water buckets and tubs, plastic

Dan's Saddlery
N. Babylon, NY

Farnam Companies Inc.
Omaha, NE

Fortex/Fortiflex
San Juan, PR

Horsemen's Pride Inc.
Ravenna, OH

K&D Plastics Inc.
Gainesville, TX

Maidware Products Inc.
Newark, OH

Miller Mfg. Co. Inc.
S. St. Paul, MN

Rubbermaid Agricultural
Products Inc.
Winchester, VA

Southwest Agri-Plastics Inc.
Carrollton, TX

Waterers, automatic

Equuspring
Lancaster, TX

Everfresh
Brownwood, TX

Franklin Equipment Co.
Monticello, IA

Hoskins Mfg. Co.
Hoskins, NE

Igloo Co.
Palmdale, CA

Ritchie Livestock Fountains
Conrad, IA

Index